The Diary...

Dericka,

I couldn't be more proud of how far you've came. Each Day you get closer & closer to realizing how great you are as a person, athlete, entertainer and Intellectual. No one truly knows how far they can go, only how far they've came, but remember it's the journey to see how far we can go that is the most exciting thing we can be a part of in life! Put in The Work and I'll Wish U The Luck! Am very very proud of you!

No Regrets Ever!

<u>The Diary</u>...

Poetry Taken From The Life Of . . .

Doug Lemon

Copyright © 2009 by Doug Lemon.

Library of Congress Control Number: 2009905609
ISBN: Hardcover   978-1-4415-4426-1
          Softcover   978-1-4415-4425-4

All rights reserved. No part of this book may be reproduced or transmitted in any form or by any means, electronic or mechanical, including photocopying, recording, or by any information storage and retrieval system, without permission in writing from the copyright owner.

This is a work of fiction. Names, characters, places and incidents either are the product of the author's imagination or are used fictitiously, and any resemblance to any actual persons, living or dead, events, or locales is entirely coincidental.

This book was printed in the United States of America.

To order additional copies of this book, contact:
Xlibris Corporation
1-888-795-4274
www.Xlibris.com
Orders@Xlibris.com
63670

TABLE OF CONTENTS

1. On Day One 14
2. **Chapter 1** The Most Beautifullest 15
3. Beautiful Sculpture #1 "Andrea" 17
4. Beautiful Sculpture #2 "Amber" 18
5. Beautiful Sculpture #3 "Jess" 19
6. Beautiful Sculpture #4 "Beth" 20
7. Beautiful Sculpture #5 "Kaitlin" 21
8. Beautiful Sculpture #6 "Brittney" 22
9. Beautiful Sculpture #7 "Kaylisha" 23
10. Beautiful Sculpture #8 "Cierra" 24
11. Beautiful Sculpture #9 "Mya" 25
12. Beautiful Sculpture #10 "Wendi" 26
13. Beautiful Sculpture #11 "NeAmbi" 27
14. Beautiful Sculpture #12 "Sophia" 28
15. Beautiful Sculpture #13 "Kirsten" 29
16. Beautiful Sculpture #14 "Kim" 30
17. Beautiful Sculpture #15 "Kristina" 31
18. Beautiful Sculpture #16 "Alexis" 32
19. Beautiful Scùlpture #17 "Stephanie" 33
20. Beautiful Sculpture #18 "Theresa" 34
21. Beautiful Sculpture #19 "Brynne" 35
22. Beautiful Sculpture #20 "Elly" 36
23. Beautiful Sculpture #21 "Michelle" 37
24. Beautiful Sculpture #22 "Macy" 38
25. Beautiful Sculpture #23 "Alyssa" 39
26. Beautiful Sculpture #24 "Julia" 40
27. Beautiful Sculpture #25 "Leah" 41
28. Beautiful Sculpture #26 "Kris" 42
29. Beautiful Sculpture #27 "Shannon" 43
30. Beautiful Sculpture #28 "Candy" 44

31. **Chapter 2** Thinking Out, When Inside The Box 45

32. Twilights 46
33. Untitled 47
34. Suffix—The Suffering After the X 48

35.	Stranger Attraction	49
36.	The Countdown to the Countdown of You Coming Back	50
37.	Choose Your Karma . . .	51
38.	Lifetime Snapshots	52
39.	Loves Many Orbits	53
40.	Simply Dedicated 2 Aaliyah Haughton	54
41.	Adoration	55
42.	Cinderella—Dedicated 2 Michelle	56
43.	360 Degrees	57
44.	If She's A Dime I'd Rather Be Broke . . .	58
45.	Something 2 think about . . .	59
46.	Destroy & Rebuild	60
47.	It's Not That I Don't Love U (Cause U Know That I Do)	61
48.	Rewind & Play Again	62
49.	"What About My Dreams?"	63
50.	Shakespeare in Love	64
51.	What Is This In My Veins	65
52.	July 9th	66
53.	**Chapter 3** Life, What's At The End?	67
54.	But You Did . . .	68
55.	Kari's Eulogy Dedicated 2 Kari	69
56.	(The Title is the Last Line)	70
57.	As 👁 Look In2 Your 👁'z	72
58.	I Know You're Still Alive, Cause . . .	73
59.	Scent of a Woman	74
60.	Our Night	75
61.	⁄N↤E↤WAY↗	76
62.	👁 Lost Hope . . .	77
63.	Y 👁 Can't C U No More—4 Kati	78
64.	How Did U Get On That Side?	79
65.	My Biggest Fear	80
66.	**Chapter 4** Otherworldly Inspired	81
67.	Untitled 2	82
68.	👁 /Just Can't Get Clean\	83
69.	Take Me With U	84
70.	Y My 👁 👁's Cry	85
71.	"Lyric"	86
72.	Parted Souls	87
73.	And Yet I Still Want You . . .	88
74.	Enter the Black Hole	89
75.	6 Feet Deep	90
76.	Is it Any Better Up There (4-2Pac)	91

77.	She Waits . . . For His Return	92
78.	Radio	95
79.	giving you a chance . . . (a daughters gift)	97
80.	Amnesia 1wonone	99
81.	to2 Amnesia twotoo	100
82.	Tres Amnesia Three . . . 3	101
83.	For Amnesia 4Four	102
84.	notes from heaven	103
85.	**Chapter 5** Songs	105
86.	Filled with Tearz	106
87.	Do "you" Love Me	108
88.	My Release Part 1	110
89.	My Release Part 2	110
90.	NYURican Fantasy	112
91.	Columbian Fantasy	113
92.	Bahamian Fantasy	114
93.	Trinidadian Fantasy	115
94.	Mexican Fantasy	116
95.	Unknown Fantasy	117
96.	Peruvian Fantasy	118
97.	Cuban Fantasy	119
98.	My Eulogy	120
99.	**Chapter 6** THE STORM . .	121
100.	Y? Can't 👁 . . . ♀"Dream	122
101.	My Time Is Almost Up	124
102.	When Will My Past Catch Up?	125
103.	My Past Is Coming	126
104.	Just Give Me The Answer	127
105.	Do Not Wake Me When Eye Dream—It's All I Have Left	128
106.	I Hate You	129
107.	Is It My Destiny (2 B Lonely)	130
108.	DEAD SOUL WALKING 1 & 2	131
109.	Dead Soul Walking 1.5	132
110.	The Rain, The Storm	133
111.	White Lady	135
112.	**Chapter 7** . . . After The Storm	137
113.	Is It My Destiny (2 B Lonely) Part Deuce	138
114.	When 👁 Rest, 👁 Now Rest in Peace . . .(So Please Let Me Sleep)	139
115.	U ease my soul	140
116.	Just Dream—4 Me	141
117.	Thanks 2 My Scars	142

118.	It's Not So Bad, It's Not So Bad	143
119.	I Saw U Behind Me In The Mirror—Dedicated 2 Hope	144
120.	Do Not Wake Me ☜ May B Free	145
121.	Sometimes ☜ Cry	146
122.	**Chapter 8** Thoughts of Love	147
123.	Maybe . . .?	148
124.	Maybe . . . (Continued & Finished)	150
125.	One More Night Z	151
126.	Love!	152
127.	Love?	152
128.	Where The Red Fern Grows	153
129.	If U Should Die	154
130.	My lil Secret	155
131.	Childhood Sweetheart	156
132.	Love Poem #1	157
133.	Love Poem #2 (Swahili)	157
134.	Love Poem # 3 (Croatian)	157
135.	Love Poem #4 (Latin)	158
136.	Love Poem #5 (Arabic)	158
137.	Love Poem # 6 (Chinese)	158
138.	Love Poem # 7 (Hindi)	159
139.	Love Poem #8 (Portuguese)	159
140.	Love Poem #9 (Russian)	159
141.	Love Poem #10 (Korean)	160
142.	Love Poem #11 (Japanese)	160
143.	Love Poem #12 (German)	160
144.	Love Poem # 13 (Italia)	161
145.	Love Poem #14 (Espanol)	161
146.	Love Poem #15 (Français)	161
147.	Love Poem #16	161
148.	& THAT'S Y I HURT . . .	162
149.	We were supposed 2 grow old 2gether but I didn't have a chance	165
150.	I wanna write U a song	166
151.	Y Don't U Want Me	167
152.	There's Nothing 4 Me Here, Except U—4 Ashlee my baby sister	168
153.	My Dreams	169
154.	Ugly Beauty 1	170
155.	Hit By A Bus	171
156.	Fake Poem #1	173
157.	Off Limits, No More	175
158.	All Stunned	176
159.	Sexiest One Ever . . .	178
160.	Ugly Beauty 2	180

161.	The Poem Version 2 (The Long Lost Version)	181
162.	Not even a start . . .	184
163.	No Introduction Needed	184
164.	'MIXED' EMOTIONS CAN BE 100% REAL	185
165.	In The Closet	187
166.	3 Strikes	188
167.	I'll wait forever . . . oo	190
168.	**Chapter 9** Thoughts To Ponder	193
169.	I believe	194
170.	What you really mean . . .	195
171.	The secret to Life, that you forgot	197
172.	The Glass is Half Empty	199
173.	The Glass Is Half Full	200
174.	Beautiful Disaster	201
175.	Beautiful Lies	202
176.	An Adopted Misconception	203
177.	a 9.5 love in '95	204
178.	more thoughts about a 9.5 love in '95	205
179.	Six Degrees of "I know you from somewhere . . ."	206
180.	I'll sleep when I'm dead!	207
181.	but now,	207
182.	My Philosophy—4 Victoria	208
183.	**Chapter 10** Stories/Spoken Word	209
184.	Story #1	210
185.	I My Downfall	211
	A. (I Had A Dream)	211
186.	Story #2	213
187.	Story #3	214
188.	II My Downfall . . . Part 2	215
	A. (I Had A Vision)	215
189.	Story #4	217
190.	Story #5	218
191.	Story #6	219
192.	Story #7	220
193.	II My Downfall	221
	B. A Second Vision	221
194.	Story #8	222
195.	Story #9	223
196.	Story #10	224
197.	Story #11	225
198.	Story #12	226

199.	**Chapter 11** Covering My Bases	227
200.	"Going Broke"	228
201.	I AM . . . (1994)	229
202.	If 👁 Should Die . . .	230
203.	u r me	231
204.	Nintendo (Tribute to Youth)	232
205.	This Life	233
206.	I Am 2005	234
207.	I'll Teach You The Most Important Thing You'll Ever Need To Know	235
208.	You've been sketched before	237
209.	My Favorite Poem	238
210.	I Don't Wanna Write Today.	239
211.	How To Write An Epic Poem	241

Dedication

To everyone I've ever loved, hated or anywhere in-between. Somewhere between the covers you've inspired or been portrayed. More personally...I would like to thank my sister Jaime, who because her poetry was so beautiful, it made me soooooo jealous that I had to start writing. My other inspirations: My baby sister Ashlee, Mrs. Marks, Theresa Angelopolous, and my parents. Thanks Jay for threatening my life if I didn't write a book. Thanks Michelle for all your patience! Last but not least, thank you Rachel Simon, Emily Souza, the voices in my head, the library and anyone else who helped with translations!

My Ten-Year Apology

The poem that started it all . . . On Day One is one of my favorites, and in many ways is my favorite. Some poems take time, and time and more time, and some are stuck in my head for years. They come out in many forms consciously or unconsciously. This poem was one of the ones that I couldn't write fast enough. My pen, and my typing, couldn't keep up with, what was coming from my head. It's one of those poems that come out exactly the way you hear it in your head, and therefore no corrections are needed. It was written a few years ago in less then 5 minutes total on a spur of the moment urge. Someone then asked me, "If you can write this in 5 minutes, why don't you write a book." I said I would and it was put on the back burner for years. Reality hit me when I realized, someone had read my stuff a few years before, and asked that same question. Finally, after being hit in the head by reality, three times in one week. I decided I wanted to apologize to those people who sincerely liked my work, and wanted me to do something with it. I felt the only way, to truly be sorry, was to make good on the multiple promises made to these people years ago. So here's my ten-year apology. I'm sorry and I hope you all accept.

ON DAY ONE

AFTER GOD PAINTED U, HE THEN CREATED
SIGHT, 4 SOMETHING THAT BEAUTIFUL MUST B
SEEN. WHEN GOD SCULPTED U HE THEN CREATED
THE SENSATION OF TOUCH, SO WHEN ONE FELT U,
THEY COULD FEEL WHAT PERFECTION IS.
WHEN GOD GAVE U A VOICE, HE THEN GAVE MAN
EARS, SO THEY COULD HEAR THE ANGELIC
VOICE THAT WOULD MELT THEIR HEARTS TIME
AND TIME AGAIN.
AS HE PUT FINISHING TOUCHES ON HIS MOST
PERFECT CREATION HE GAVE U DARK BEAUTIFUL
HAIR. NEXT HE KNEW HE MUST CREATE
THE SENSE OF SMELL, SO WHEN ONE
PUT HIS HEAD ON THE SIDE OF YOUR
CARAMEL NECK, HE WOULD ALSO SMELL YOUR BEAUTY.
HE THEN PUT LUSCIOUS LIPS ON HIS CREATION,
THAT WE NOW CALL A QUEEN,
AND DECIDED HE MUST THEN CREATE TASTE, OR EVEN
WITH ALL HIS OTHER CREATIONS MAN COULD
NEVER APPRECIATE YOUR TOTAL WORTH.
WITH ONE LAST ADDITION
HE GAVE MAN A HEART
A GIFT 2 U,
4 MAN 2 USE,
2 SHOW HIS APPRECIATION
4 A MASTERPIECE
THAT WILL NEVER BE OUTDONE.

Chapter 1

<u>The Most Beautifullest</u>

I know what your thinking. Where's the spell check? Well that's the problem, to me that's everything that's wrong with this world. We're told as kids not to handle problems ourselves. We're told to find an adult. However if we do that more than once, we're a tattletale . . . How can we learn from a person, who can make something so simple, turn into something so difficult? If you can't explain to me what's right or wrong, how can you explain to me what beauty is?

Keith Murray had an album named "The Most Beautifullest." Though I couldn't tell you for sure what made him name his album that, or even what the title meant to him. But for me it's meaning is simple. Beauty isn't always perfection. Beauty isn't perfection. Are we really attracted to what's perfect on someone or by what makes them unique and different? One hundred similar traits shared among one hundred different people is enough to give everyone a combination that makes them truly unique. Give a thousand more traits to those same 100 people and you have something closer to the world we live in.

For me to single someone out of a crowd and say, "That is beauty," is not only an incorrect statement, but its also very close-minded, to think beauty can be summed up in one picture, one definition. Most Beautifullest may be an imperfect term to some, but it's beauty is in the fact that one knows it's incorrect yet felt most beautiful wasn't enough to describe the beauty they saw in front of them. Why is there more than one type of painting, more than one genre of music, more than one sport or type of dance to watch or display? Cause beauty comes in many forms. "The Most Beautifullest" is every imperfection/perfection that you see around you. It's an imperfection only if you choose not to see the beauty in it . . . Witness beauty and everything becomes more beautiful.

These poems are called beautiful sculptures. Each sculpture has a name to go with it. The name is not necessarily named after a particular person. It is more of a reference, for me the author, and you the reader to be on the same page if you have a question about it. That way you can say "Julia," and I would have a better chance of knowing which poem you are talking about, then if you had said #24. It is important for you to remember that if you find a poem that fits you, or a particular person it reminds you of, it is no longer named "Krystal," "Kris" or "Elly" for you. It then takes on the name of your choice. Names are only a reference for my memory. Names will change for your memory, as they apply to your beautiful sights.

BEAUTIFUL SCULPTURE #1 AKA "ANDREA"

CHOCOLATE MILK LADY,
FILLED TO THE BRIM.
BREATHTAKING & ADDICTIVE,
MY VIRGINIA SLIM.
EYES STARING BACK,
LIKE STARS IN THE NIGHT.
& THEM RED WINE LIPS,
THAT LOOK READY TO BITE.
ONE ON ONE THOUGHTS,
FOR AN ATHENA PHYSIQUE.
& THOSE LONG-STEM ROSES,
DOWN TO YOUR FEET.
INDEPENDENT MINDS,
YET WE MAKE EACH OTHER THINK.
THOUGHTS HARDER THAN LIQUOR,
THAT I'VE BEEN YEARNING TO DRINK.

Beautiful Sculpture #2 AKA "Amber"

Face Of An Angel,
Cinnamon Skin,
Licorice Whipped
So Sweet & Thin.
Light & Dark,
Half 151,
1 Glass Of You
Makes My Body Numb.
A Glance Deep Inside,
Your Bedroom Eyes,
Makes Our Souls Collide
As Our Temperatures Rise.
4-Ever Mi Amor,
Are Whispers That's Been Said,
2 A Perfect Girl
2 Hot 2 Get Out Of My Head.

Beautiful Sculpture #3 AKA "Jess"

Eyes So Blue
I Can See The Ocean Inside
With Hair Silky & Blonde
Down To Your Side
Ready Whip Soft
Whip Cream Smooth
Eyes Ask The Question
Walk Speaks The Truth
Heels Take The Step
Legs Take The Stride
Thighs Make It Glide
Catches Every Single Eye
Cool Summer Lips Or
A Warm Winter Kiss
Paralyzing "Fantasy" Beauty
Closes Eyes & Sets U Adrift

"BETH" AKA BEAUTIFUL SCULPTURE #4

VANILLA FLAVORED KISS
WITH A CUTE LIL GRIN
SOFTEST LIL TOUCH FROM YOUR
MACADAMIA SKIN
TIGER-EYE HAIR POLISHED
SMOOTH LIKE NEW ORLEANS JAZZ
SPELLBINDING EYES OF
DEEP SMOKEY TOPAZ
SIX-PACK STOMACH
AND A CONFIDENT SWAG
MARSHMALLOW BOOTY &
HIPS THAT ROCK & SWAY
LIPS COOL TO THE TOUCH
SWEET LIKE SUGAR IN THE RAW
ONE OF THE MOST STUNNING, &
GORGEOUS GIRLS I EVER SAW

Beautiful Sculpture #5 AKA "Kaitlin"

C the Sunrise
On Your Sunset Skin
Golden Heart
Eyes Precious Gems
Dolled Up from
Fingers 2 Your Toes
Runway Walk &
Your Attitude is Swoll
Soft 2 the Touch
& Some Cherry Lips
Strawberry Tongue
Make a Skittle₃ Kiss
Eyes So Bright, I
Can C U In The Dark
They Make Cupid Strike
Bullets Through Your Heart

Beautiful Sculpture #6
AKA
"Brittney"

Eyes Glistening Ice
Canvas Caramel
Decisive Figure
Essence Unparallel
Siren Stares With
Eyelashes That Flutter
Body & Butters
That Can Make U Stutter
Lips That Converse
Makes Heart Rate Steeper
Personality Is Real
Beauty's Even Deeper
Masterpiece Mold
That Stays On Beat
Caramel Thighs
R A Catwalk Treat
Surprising Washboard
On Roller Coaster Curves
Tried This Once B4
A Sculpture 2 Good 4 Words

"Kaylisha" AKA Beautiful Sculpture #7

Honey-Gold Mami
Sticky & Sweet
Minnie Mouse Eyelashes
Mini Sized Feet
Innocent Smile
On Your Babyface
Honeydew Melons
Tiny Little Waist
Sweet Little Whisper
From Plump Ripe Lips
Tells Me To Taste
Your Nectar Fingertips
Every Word You Say
Brings Chills Down My Spine
Babygirl, Senorita, Mamacita
Ages Better Than Wine

Beautiful Sculpture #8 AKA "Cierra"

Innocent Illusion
Brown Sugar Baby
Devilish Delusion
Mixture Perfect Lady
Picture Perfect Beauty
Good Enough To Eat
Cute Lil—
Absolute Style Of Petite
Sizzling Playful Smile
With A Bite Of Your Lips
Sugar Cane Neck
Pure Enough To Lick
Masterpiece So Complete
Designed With The Best
Senorita In The Streets
Fill In The Rest...
Recognize Shortie
Skin Spicy & Sweet
Babygirl Sporty
What A Visual Treat

Beautiful Sculpture #9 AKA "Mya"

Maple Skin Dame
Pure & Untapped
Emerald Eyes
Classic Treasure Map
Gold Treasure Chest Hidden
Bullion Booty Unfound
Smile That's Sweet
& Speaks Profound
Jell-O Shot Curves
Softer Than Mink
Fingernails That
Dig, Scratch & Sink
Babygirl Free Spirited &
Down 2 Earth
2 Many Beauties 2 Even B Found
In This Woman's Worth

"Wendi" AKA "Beautiful Sculpture #10"

Curls Set Ablaze
Hot Inferno Locks
Earthquake Beauty
Complete With Aftershocks
Snow White Skin
Can Make Your Body Shiver
Eyes Warm U Up
Makes Your Liver Quiver
Unspeakable Voice
Shares Secrets Whispered
Either Drops Your Chin
Or Makes U Kiss Her
Secrets Just 4 Me &
Secrets Just 4 U
She Makes Your Body Freeze
& Your Lips Turn Blue

Beautiful Sculpture #11 AKA "NeAmbi"

Classy Lady &
Classic Beauty
Milk Chocolate Complexion
When Stirred It Moves Me
Vintage Soul With An
Old School Heart
A Girl That Can Make
Your Heart Stop . . . Or Start
Bona Fide & Immaculate Lady?
Or Flawless Just A Thought?
Or Being Sent,
Everything You Ever Sought?
Lassie Composed With A Joking Smile
Or An Intelligent Gaze
Beautiful Dame To Remember
For A Lifetime, And A Day

Beautiful Sculpture #12 AKA "Sophia"

Galaxy Eyez,
Infinite w/ A Sparkling Beam
Smoothest Skin Ever Seen,
A Sweet, Dark, Chocolate Dream
Plum Colored,
Delicate, Peach Soft Lips
Perfection Is Your Waist
Meshing w/ Your Pillow Like Hips
Voice Off Your Tongue
Makes Knees Weak & Bent
Innocent Smile Towards Me
Trumps N-E Fant-A-C I Ever 'Dreamt'

"Kirsten" AKA Beautiful Sculpture #2

Red Sand Beach Skin
2 Run Through Your Palms
Ocean Breeze Off Your Smile
Warms, Cools, & Calms
Ripe Mango Lips &
Tahitian Pearl Eyes
Make Pulses Rise
Like A Midnight Tide
Hair Beautifully Unique
Strands Of Black Coral Reef
You Make Heart Rates Steep
& Souls Feel Complete

Beautiful Sculpture #14 AKA "Kim"

Irreplaceable Onyx Eyes &
Ebony Silk String Hair.
Beautiful Cherry Blossom Elegance
Makes Glances, Stare . . .
More Sizzling Than A Dragons Blow
With Some Intoxicating Sake Lips
Make For A Kiss
Hotter Than Wasabi Can Give
More Striking Than A Samurai's Sword
& More Graceful Than A Katakana Stroke
Bijin Baby Had Me At . . .
Well, Before You Even Spoke

Beautiful Sculpture #15 AKA "Kristina"

Beauty In The Breeze
Ethnicity Unknown
Butterscotch Skin
Perfectly Toned
Magic Brown Eyes
Trailblazing Gaze
Succulent Legs That
Can Walk 4 Days
Sexxling Hot Rising 2 A
Bead Of Sweat
Sparkling Smile Can
Make You A Nervous Wreck
Scent I Can't Remember
Yet I'll Never Forget.
The Most Memorable Girl
I Never Met...

"Alexis" AKA Beautiful Sculpture #16

Glimmering Bella
Cotton Candy Hips
Ocean Pearl Smile
On Guava Colored Lips
Cocoanut Curves, On Beautiful
White Ocean Sand Skin
Softest, Most Delicate Voice
That Takes My Wind
Shoulders Touching Platinum Silk
Shoots Goosebumps Through My Skin
Breathtaking Eyes, Leaves
My Lungs Collapsed Again
Mysterious Elegance
Exposing Intimate Glow
Crème De La Crème
The New Millenniums Marilyn Monroe

Beautiful Sculpture #17 A.K.A. "Stephanie"

Brown Haired Girl, With
Champagne Skin
Egyptian Cotton Tresses
Glide In The Wind
Pearly White Bites
Couples Ebony Olive Eyes
Pure Unfiltered Voice, Beauty
You Can't Hide Or Disguise
Watermelon Lips Climax, A
Sugary Sweet Face
Makes You Wonder, How
That Smiles Tastes
A Honey Dipped Stuffoli Dessert,
Crème Brulèe Baby With Tiramisu,
Don't Forget The Cannoli
And Sweet Melting Fondue

or

Brown Haired Girl, With
Champagne Skin
Egyptian Cotton Tresses
Glide In The Wind
Pearly White Bites
Couples Jaded Olive Eyes
Pure Unfiltered Voice, Beauty
You Can't Hide Or Disguise
Watermelon Lips Climax, A
Sugary Sweet Face
Makes You Wonder, How
That Smiles Tastes
A Honey Dipped Stuffoli Dessert,
Crème Brulèe Baby With Tiramisu,
Don't Forget The Cannoli
And Sweet Melting Fondue

Beautiful Sculpture #18 AKA "Theresa"

Aphrodite Angel
Olive Oil Skin
Almond Eyes, With
A Honey Dipped Grin
Lightning Bolts Strikes
Your Goddess-Like Hips
Your Soft Gelato Lips
Make For A Melting Kiss
Stimulating Intellectual
Plato, Socrates, & Aristotle
& Your Profile Can Match
The Worlds Supermodels
Body Sculpted To Perfection, Like
The Coliseum, It Stands Through Time
& Your Personality Persistently
Appreciates Like Wine

"Brynne" AKA Beautiful Sculpture S19

Beignet Baby,
Candy Yam Sweet
Hypnotizing Hook.
Your Melody Speaks . . .
Kaleidoscope Locks
Jolly-Rancher Streaks
Personality & Hair, More Colorful
Than The Great Barrier Reef
Angelic Voice
Makes My Heart Stop With Time
Funny How When You Speak,
Your Breath Always Takes Mine
Everything About You
Gives Me Fever & Chills
You Buckle My Knees, &
Make My Memories Stand Still

Beautiful Sculpture #20 AKA "Elly"

Magma Hot Mami, With
Black Sand Beach Hair
Red Hot Lava Streaks
Touching Shoulders Bare
Piercing, Stabbing Eyes
Give A Penetrating Look
Sheer Frame With Generous Curves
Has Everybody Shook
Graceful Motions
Hips, Lips, Fingertips
100 Proof Bliss
Invigorates Any Kiss
Beauty So Clean, It
Makes You St-St-Stutter
Skin So Soft & Smooth
I Can't Believe It's Not Butter

Beautiful Sculpture #21 AKA "Michelle"

Hurricane Hottie
Beaming Off The Ocean
Heat-Wave Mami, With
Fluid Liquid Motion
Daiquiri Lips & A
Nectarine Neck
Invigorated Licuor Kiss
Sweetened With Triple Sec
Deep Sea Wonder
& Coastline Splashes
Cool Down The Heat, From
Your Beach Fire Ashes
Sunset Beauty
Pineapple Sweet
Tantalizing Temptation
A Tropical Treat

"Macy" AKA Beautiful Sculpture #22

Snowflake Beauty, Creates
Snow Storm Emotions
Wind Chill Whispers, Generates
Blizzard Notions
Moonlight Belle
Custard Smooth Curves
Diamond Filled Eyes, With
Body Language Words
Strong Silk Strands, With
Cotton Candy Strips
Nude Shoulders & Back
With Rich Sponge Hips
Strawberry Rose Cheeks
Sapphire Pink Lips
Love & Desire Sealed
With A Peppermint Kiss

Beautiful Sculpture #23 AKA "Alyssa"

Cocoa Brown Tone, To
A Toffee Shade
Sweet, Soft, And Smooth
Like Fresh Marmalade
Steep Mountain Curves
Amusement Park Twists
Hydraulic Walk, Gives
Multiple Places To Kiss
Ammolite Eyes
That Transform Sporadically
Infinite Bodily Wonders, You
Couldn't Solve Mathematically
Pure Loveliness Revealed
Through An Era Of Events
Assets Minuscule Though Immense
No Doubt Heaven Sent

Beautiful Sculpture #24 AKA "Julia"

Fine, Fragile Features;
Sensitive Neck, Slim & Steep
Amidst Ravishing Radiant Skin
Vixen Complete & Vertically Sleek
Possessing Galaxy Attributes
Your Rays Melt Ice
With Lines Exquisite,
Pure, Poetic & Precise
Legs Luscious, Lustrous & Lean
Conjoins Detailed, Delicate Thighs
Creating A Supreme,
Glistening, Graceful Stride
Glance At A Tantalizing
Teeny, Abdominal Treat
Upon Curves Slight, Elusive
Yet Elegant Furthermore Elite
Expectations Of Excellence
Accordingly You Appear,
Axis Tilts, Torques, & Turns
Completes A Show Sharp & Sheer

"Leah" AKA Beautiful Sculpture #25

White Wine Skin
Outlined Perky & Flawless
Sexiness From Eyes To Toes,
Should Be Lawless
Flirtatious Shoulder, Shoots
Ripples Through My Veins
Lip Walks A Runway
Makes My Heart Beat Insane
Imagination Lets Me Swim & Explore
Your Infinite Eyes Of The Sea
Our Tectonic Plates Fuse
Making Em-Oceans Run Deep
Heat Rises On The Horizon
A Heart-Stopping Sight Since Birth
You're Either Where Fantasy Meets Reality
Or Where Heaven, Meets Earth

BEAUTIFUL SCULPTURE #26 AKA "KRIS"

CARNIVOROUS EYES
YOU'RE THE EYE THE STORM
CURVES MAKE A PERFECT EXHIBIT
FOR YOUR ARTISTIC FORM
THE DE VINCI OVER THE SHOULDER
THE PICASSO COMPLEXION
THE GRAFFITI ARMS,
TAGGED TO PERFECTION
A TONED SCULPTURE FRAME
MOLDS A 3D SKETCH
VAN GOGH ON THE BACK, WITH
MEMOIRS ON THE NECK
YOU MAKE PHEROMONES GO WILD
& DOPAMINE INCREASE
YOU'RE A PLETHORA OF BEAUTY
THAT FAILS TO CEASE

Beautiful Sculpture #27 AKA "Shannon"

A Sight To Be Seen
Your Grin Looks At Me
Question Mark Curves
Can Banish You From Reality
She Can Stand Her Own
Tough Yet Smooth & Soft
You Make Dreaming Fun
& Make Me Turn & Toss
Perfect Personality & Aura
Just Where It Begins
Cheeks, Neck & Back
Hair, Stomach & Skin
Legs, Lips & Hips
.Reasons Everyone Remembers Ya
Smile, Thighs, Eyes
Etc.,
Et Cetera,
"   " . . .

Beautiful Sculpture #28 AKA "Candy"

Bon-Bon Bella
Bubblicious Belle
Butterscotch Beauty
With A Sweet Candy Shell
Sugar Babie Lady
Licorice Laced Locks
Lemon Drop From Heaven
My Psychedelic Lollipop
Tantalizing Taffy Tongue
Makes Sweetened Starburst Words
Carmel Apple Cutie w/
Fluid Coca-Cola Curves
Candy Cane Clavicle
& A Now & Later Neck
Kool-Aid Infused Lips
Make Hawaiian Punch Pecks
Red Hot, Hot Tamale
Suits A Jolly Rancher Tongue
Butterfinger, Peanut Butter Cup
My Delicious Cinnabon
Mounds of Almond Joy
The Sweetest Sorbet
Rich Truffle Skin
Soft, Smooth Milky Way
A Sweet Candy Heart
Creates Jujyfruit Bliss
To Put A Ring Pop On Your Finger
& Give A Sweet Hershey's Kiss

Chapter 2

Thinking out, when Inside the Box

Here's what I call assignment poetry. *To be creative within guidelines. You must do this, but you have free reign.* It makes no sense yet tons at the same time. So By Haiku, Concrete or Shakespearian style, I've tried to use all forms. Some come from the left side of the brain, some from the right, while I truly have no idea where the rest are derived.

Twilights

Traveling in afterthoughts of my origin
I exit the highway to travel
I traveled out the door gathering after-
       thoughts in my notebook
The afterthoughts had traveled to the
       exit of the highway

Untitled

Talking to death through my window
I see the sky
The window picks me to say goodbye
Who is that talking in my window tonight
Who is that sinking in the sky
I borrow twisted lies to talk
I exchange flowers for death
The window is twisted the window lies
I pick a lie to journey
The window tells lies, lies
Does the window lie or will I borrow death tonight

Suffix–The Suffering After the X

Karing U **Ka**me
Karing U Were Not
Kareful With My Heart
Kareful U Were Not
Karefree <u>When I was with U</u>, but
Karefree U Were With Me
Kareful With My Soul
Cause I Care 4 U A Lot
I Paint A Perfect Picture
Karrots Filled With Rocks
A **Kar**riage That Contains Us
But A **Kar**icature Is What The Artist Jots
More Make Believe Than Real
Should Be **Kar**eful What Your Heart Feels
And It Hurts That U Sung A **Kar**ol With Your Mouth
When No **Kar**es Is What U Sought

This is a poem for everyone who ever was dating someone, and then all of a sudden to your, amazement your dream girl/guy steps into your life. Now this person not only walks into your life, but they notice you! On top of that, this person makes it very clear that they want you to know, that they noticed you as you noticed them. Now as you get slightly caught up in the moment you remember that, "I'm taken." And in your head you can only say "You gotta be kidding me?" Well from a Haiku style poem format (5-7-5 syllables) and a Hawaiian word that can mean two different things (Hi or Goodbye). You can end the poem the way you want to. You can choose to end it the right way (remember it's easier to say then do when the situation unfolds in front of you.) If you've been through this before, you know exactly what was going through my mind at the time. If you haven't . . . yet . . . Good luck when it happens to you! The attraction to a stranger can be more overwhelming then you think, no matter if you choose to end the story or start a story.

Stranger Attraction

Is it "Hi" or "Bye?"
We met, yet we're passing by
Aloha gorgeous

The Countdown to the Countdown of You Coming Back

Nine Strikes On The Clock
Creates 8 Crazy Ideas,
7 Lucky Thoughts &
6 Reasons Why
5 Minutes
Be4 You Leave, Cause
Three Seasons Won't Change
Two Hearts Creating
One Love

Choose Your Karma . . .

**Love Perfected Kills Thoughts Bad
But
Bad Thoughts Kills Perfected Love**

LIFETIME SNAPSHOTS

Memories
Sexy Sweet
Lasting Lusting Loving
Time Seems To Stop
Moments

LOVES MANY ORBITS

STUDY LOVES FORCE,
FORCE STUDIES LOVE,
FORCE OF LOVES ORBIT
DISTANCE LOVES FORCE.
LOVE ORBITS FORCE,
FORCE DISTANCE LOVE,
ORBIT LOVES FORCE OR
FORCE A DISTANT ORBIT.

Simply Dedicated 2 Aaliyah Haughton

Angelic

Amazing

Lovely

Intelligent

Youthful

Alluring

Heavenly

Adoration

Lady Love Dies
Honey, Distance Love
Love Discovers Lady
Discovers Honey Love
Lady Models Love
Lady, Love, Love

Cinderella -Dedicated 2 Michelle

Touch my soul
Over and over
Time seems to stop
Aching while your away, yet
Lonely no more
Love fills my heart
You bring me joy

I smile deep inside
Never as happy as now

Little things
Overflow my body
Vintage
Everlasting love

360 Degrees

And then U came
B4 my 👁's
Completing my smile
Dawning a new day
Everlasting love
Flying away
Gone 4ever

If She's A Dime I'd Rather Be Broke . . .

Your outfit is a comical joke,
And you smell like stale smoke,
    Yet your nose is up all the time
    But girl if you think you're a dime,
I'd honestly rather be broke . . .

Something 2 think about . . .

THINGS MAY NEVER WORK OUT
THINGS MAY NEVER BE *PERFECT*

PERFECT TIMES MAY COME
PERFECT MAY HAPPEN IN OUR *EYES*

EYES THAT STIMULATED INSTANT ATTRACTION
EYES IN MUTUAL *SATISFACTION*

SATISFACTION ENOUGH FOR FRIENDS
SATISFACTION ONLY WORKS IN COMPROMISE & *RETRACTION*

RETRACTION FOR LUST & INFATUATION? I CALLED YOU
    BABY
RETRACTION FOR LOVE & FRIENDSHIP? I CALLED YOU *LADY*

LADY THAT I WANT TO KNOW MORE ABOUT
LADY NOW YOU TELL ME WHAT YOU'RE ABOUT

Destroy & Rebuild

Promises, Perpetuating Poetry r Powerful Pistols Poppin Problems Persuaded by People Perpetrating Peaceful Plot-Filled Situations, Psychotic Salutations Single-handedly Serving Simple-Minded Solutions while Scraping Skin Irritations, Instantly Immobilizing Infinite Irrational Illusions Inducing Images of Insanity Implicating Infatuations Masking what Matters Mutual Mysteries not Multiple Manipulations

It's Not That I Don't Love U
(Cause U Know That I Do)

You Know I Love U
So Please Don't Ask If I Do
Loves Not The Problem
& It Never Was 4 U
It's Just Well, I Don't Like U

Rewind & Play Again

Secrets whispered as I leave
Walk back up the steps
Your scents all over me
It leaves and goes back to your sheets
Morning turns back to night
And we wake back up
Exhausted in bed again
As we gain energy from our adrenaline
Sweat slowly dries back up
Body temperature rises
We feel again, for the first time
Multiple sexy surprises
We shoulda been doing this
Another nights first kiss
Sure you wanna do this
Eyes signal possible bliss
Gotta leave as I arrive
Can't wait to see you soon
You ask "What you doing tonight?"
Can tell it's your call from the light
You hang up
I'll call you back at a quarter to ten
Are you all talk or what
We ever gonna see each other again?
"Man I haven't heard from you in awhile"
As we talk daily more and more
What's your name, I like your style
I Know I've seen you somewhere before
& That's how we become friends
Second time as strangers our paths cross
If it's meant we'll see each other again
My first glimpse of you gets me lost

What about my dreams? Interesting as a kid your full of dreams. Some dreams seem very out of reach and some are only out of reach cause we're too afraid to fail. Funny how the younger you are the less afraid you are to fail. Also when you have a problem it's funny how the best advice is the most simplified. Simplified? A big word to just say easy. Well next time you need an advice without all the extra b.s. everyone else will give you. Ask a kindergartner, they'll make it a yes no answer. So what about my dreams what about yours? What's the problem? Well tell the problem, ask the question. Two syllables to answer the question yourself. Any more and your trying to manipulate yourself.

"What About My Dreams?"

Sleepy
Tengo Sueno
Tired & I Hate My Job
This Isn't What I Want To Do
Quitting

Shakespeare in Love

Shhh. Close your eyes now. I will see you soon.
I stare at the stars. I stare at the walls.
They offer me little comfort here.
I sit here waiting for something distant.
You tell me many things, but don't tell much.
You tell me truth, and how you really feel,
Only while admitting your holding back.
Give me something real, to tell me you're not.
Or I shall assume, your fate scares you too.
So let me sleep, so I'll have one less night.
One more day passes til your arrival.
Sill not easier than yesterday was.
But with yesterday and night gone for good,
I'll never have to go through it again.
You give me life's greatest gift to behold.
A promise, that must comply with our fate.
Promises that cannot be guaranteed.
Only to make sure I live while waiting.
To give me something to look forward too,
So I don't sleep through life waiting for you.

WHAT IS THIS IN MY VEINS

Adoration
Feverish Frantic
Confusion Frustration Irritation
Complete Loss of Patience
Love

JULY 9TH

|\Time is the only thing that will tell us, what will eventually, be/a|
.		c
n		c
w		o
o		p
n		a
k		n
n		y
u		i
l		n
l		g
i		o
t	_____	u
s/are background and pose the but both, us contain will It. frame\r

Chapter 3

<u>Life, What's At The End?</u>

You will constantly come into situations that may end better or worse than you had hoped for. Sometimes you look back and say, "Wow I didn't see that coming," or "Who woulda thought!" Sometimes you just get caught in headlights with disbelief on what you imagined what was going to happen. Sometimes you just gotta roll with it and keep moving forward . . .

But You Did . . .

I thought no one could make me smile
But you did . . .
I thought no one could make me laugh
But you did . . .
I thought no one listened to me when I
talked
But you did . . .
I thought no one understood me
But you did . . .
I thought no one cared about me
But you did . . .
I would always have such a bad day I'd think
no one could make me happy
But you did . . .
No one would laugh at my jokes
But you did . . .
No one ever kept their promises
But you did . . .
No one meant so much to me
But you did . . .
I didn't think you loved me too
But you did . . .
You said your love would never die
But you did . . .

Kari's Eulogy Dedicated 2 Kari

U came 2 me + U saved me
      My Queen 2 B
           👁 saw and learned what love was
👁 felt my heart Beat 4 the first
      time from the moment I met U
Problem is, is that it hasn't stopped
      And it only beats 4 U
👁 have put others in my heart
      and loved with all 👁 have
           but even with that, my heart
                beats waiting 2 feel your blood again
U left and Just like U saved me
      👁 now need some-1 2 save
           me from your aftermath
U Left me twice and at times 👁
      want a third
But your not good 4 Me A cancer that
      Kills me slowly
Every time 👁 think of U 👁 hurt
👁 don't wanna hurt anymore
So Now I gotta spread your ashes
No you're not dead, just dead 2 me
If you're no longer living maybe 👁 can move on
But it's actually the reminiscing that hurts my soul
And since U chose yourself 2 leave me here
All that's left 4 me 2 Do is Read This Eulogy
So Finally, As many Keep memories when 1 Becomes deceased
U May Live on But May our Memories Rest
      In Peace

(The Title is the Last Line)

So I'm walking down the street,
And I see this very, very, very average girl
If that,
Wearing a really cute outfit, right.
So I'm looking at this maybe average girl,
Who I have absolutely have no interest in,
walking towards me, in a cute black shirt
that has black mesh trim in kind of peasant style
yet with an edge to it
completed with silver mirage lettering on it.
She also has perfect fitting jeans for her body type
Which is something,
that seems to be a little different lately.
Plus she's got a matching handbag,
and probably the only shoes in the world,
that would match the shirt.
So by taste or mistake
I gotta admit she actually has a pretty cute ensemble on
So as she gets closer
I chose to give her a compliment
On an outfit that is well put together
Because, Well that's just who I am
So as she gets with in talking distance I say
"I love your outfit, it's cute" and I continue to walk
She looks at me in disgust
Looking me up & down like I asked her
If I could take them off
She replies before she passes me
Smacking her lips and saying
"I don't know you"
Like I was trying to get her number and
All I can think of is "I said your outfit was cute,
Not you" but I don't care
I'm just happy she can put together some thing that
Takes attention away from her face.
But I say that in my head not out loud,

Cause well that's just the type of person I am.
So I throw my empty bottle of juice away
And take my few steps back to the bus stop
And there she is waiting for the same bus.
So she answers her cell phone talking to her friend
Telling her that all these guys are hitting on her again today
As she glances my way
And that she's too good for all of them and that's why
She's single. Cause in her words "She's a dime and
She needs someone as fine as she is
To appreciate her and take care of her
Because" she says again "I'm a dime"
This time rolling her eyes as she glances my way.
Lightly shaking my head at the ground with a smile,
I then turned to the person next to me and said
Politely with a slight laugh
"If She's A Dime" [smacking my lips] "I'd Rather Be Broke . . ."

As 👁 Look In2 Your 👁'z

As 👁 Look In2 Your 👁'z 👁 C . . .
Beauty on levels 👁've never seen B4,
As 👁 Look In2 Your 👁'z 👁 C . . .
Deep inside your Soul
As 👁 Look In2 Your 👁'z 👁 C . . .
Love looking back at me
As 👁 Look In2 Your 👁'z 👁 C . . .
Picture. Perfect. Future.
As 👁 Look In2 Your 👁'z . . .
All 👁 Can Think About, Is
How Much 👁 Miss U.

I Know You're Still Alive, Cause . . .

I know you're still alive,
Through life you've always, just gotten by.
Barely working when you work.
Don't care if things are done right,
    Or get done at all.
No stress,
No high blood pressure,
No clotted veins.
Leaching every chance you get, &
Only get what's handed to you.
Only get mad by things not put in your hands,
Or if you don't want to open your palm, to receive them.
No parachute mishap,
No motorcycle flip,
Never torn to pieces by a shark,
Or mauled by a stalking bear.
You escape harm, cause you take no chances.
I don't have to read the obituaries,
To know your still alive somewhere.
I know you're still alive . . .
Cause only the good die young,
And you're not that good.

SCENT OF A WOMAN

Love Spell or Fruity & Bright
Make my body collapse
Vanilla or Cocoa Butter
Make me want to pull you close
Coconut or Guava
And I want to run my finger through your hair
Strawberries or Honey
Make me think about tasting you
Cool Water or Eternity
And I can't hold back . . . however
Chanel & Clinique
And I have to push you away
Very Sexy & Heavenly
And I have to say no
Honeysuckle & Irresistible Apple
Puts a hole in my heart
Cause Gucci & Angel
Reminds me, as you lean in to kiss me
Of You & The Girl you introduced
Cause the second scent's . . . your girlfriend's

Our Night

It started with this day
The plans we made
The time we spent
Fate didn't put us there that day
But it put us there that night
A strange turn of coincidences
Put a twist on something
Already corkscrewed
But now here it is
Something bound by fate
A moment long in awaiting
Long in the making
But in one last coil & a loop
It didn't happen cause
I knew deep inside
This wouldn't just B our first night
Fate would have made it
Our last night 2 . . .

↙N ←E ← WAY ↗

You tell me there's a method
        To accomplish what you have.
I tell you those are my goals
        Plus I have more.

You tell me this is the course I must take
I have to run on this track
There is one route to go
This is the path to follow
Watch my bearings and stay on point
This is the only road that will take me there

But U 4 got 1 thing,
👁'm smarter than U . . .
👁'd like 2 C U on top,
But U never made it here.

👁 Lost Hope . . .

Made by an idiot
Made by a racist
Made by the careless
Made by those who could care less
The smart plan 4 the not
Plan 4 the time that's right
Plan till it's 2 late
So the dumb take it in their hands
The irresponsible
The 1's that can barely help themselves
Make and run away
Make and never know
You don't need a license
You don't need $money$
You don't even need to be mentally stable
To make a life
Yet 👁 know thirty people with @ least 2 kids
Less than 10 are in control of their own life
And about 4 can handle another
You ask me Y 👁 lost hope
Cause these kids start with very little

Y 👁 Can't C U No More—4 Kati

It's True
In Many Ways
You're Like A Sister 2 Me
With Times I'll Never 4Get
Your Daughter
Brings Joy 2 Me
A Smile I'm Always Glad
2 Have Met
When I Hold Her
In My Arms, At Times
She Feels Like Mine
Smiles Appear On My Face
Until I Have 2 Leave
When I Look In2 Your Eyes
Reality Isn't Always What I C
When I C U & Your Baby
I C Your Sister
& The Daughter
We Once Seemed Destined 2 Have

How Did U Get On That Side?

I never liked the look
You walk by and I shake my head
Talent chosen to be wasted
I see you everywhere
It's like a sad story that is being told to everyone
Sad cause everyone's telling it in their eyes
It used to make me laugh
Then after time it was disgusting
Followed by sadness
Everywhere I go I see it.
Talent being ignored
But I never saw it here . . .
Until now
How the hell did you get on this side of the mirror?

My Biggest Fear

I Worry About Teaching You Right
I Worry About Not Teaching You Wrong
I Worry About Buying You Everything You Need
I Worry About Cleaning Cuts You Bleed
I Worry About Spending Enough Time With You
I Worry About Your First Day At School
I Worry About Teachers, Teaching You Lies
I Worry About Boys, And What They Might Try
I Worry About How Much Peer-Pressure Will Exist
I Worry About Anything Important I Might Miss
I Worry About Your Health
I Worry About Friendships And Wealth
But My Biggest Worry
And My Biggest Fear
Is That You Will Never Appear

Chapter 4

OTHERWORLDLY INSPIRED

Otherworldly inspired means they came from another place. I did write these poems, but I can't fully take credit for them. For when I wrote them, I felt as if I was ghostwriting through someone. I have no idea what made me write these. When I read them, I do remember writing them, but cannot tell you exactly what I was feeling while I was writing them. Maybe it was you thinking something, that you, needed, to be written. Either way I know these poems aren't just meant for me. I wasn't the only person that they were written for.

Untitled 2

Dormant It Stays
Hidden Indefinitely
If U Care U Will C
Look In My Eyes
2 C The Love I Built, 4
U Inside
The Walls May Fall
But The Foundation
Will Always Stand
Which May Turn 2 Ruins
But There 4 Eternity

👁 /Just Can't Get Clean\
—From The Song

Crying Tearz of Pain Make Me 4get
Neglect 2 Remember
That U Will Walk In The Heavens
Through My Pain,
I Wait 4 U 2 Walk Through My Door
As I Stare Close
Tired
U Exit <u>My</u> Heaven
Into <u>Yours</u>
Wait 4 Me
Exit My Life
Walk Into The Light
Goodnight
I Love You

      —Dedicated 2 The Words That
          R Spoken The Last Time
          U Hold Someone

Take Me With U

👁 C U struggle 4 breath
👁 struggle 2
Your eyes stay closed
& tears blind me 2
You're so close 2 me
Yet U feel so far away
Don't leave this world
It still needs U here
You're in pain
👁'm in pain
So if U have 2 go . . .
Take me with U

Y My 👁 👁's Cry

People ashamed of their heritage
    Cause of things their parents say
The baby has no milk
    And the father's out to play
The kids beatin' by some scum
    While the mother watches
A girl raped by three others
    She begs but they don't stop it
The kindergartner trapped in a fire
    Even though all the while his location was known
The 8-year old running the house
    Taking care of her 2 year old brother alone
Pregnant teenagers
    Who think it's normal and no big thing
The little girl that cries
    Cause it's the first time she's been told she was good at anything
The Jump Ropes that stop
    When bullets start to fly
Societies low standards
    And teachers that oblige
The little boy lying on the floor
    Because of a stray shot
Kids with disabilities
    Cause their mothers did everything but pot
The 16 year old on the corner
    Cause she thinks that's all she can do
The mom with a stillborn son
    And the one she lost in her womb

"Lyric"

U wrote a song
But the hook hurts
We used 2 make beats
Play chords & flirt
Beautiful music was made
But never a verse
I didn't write this lyric
But I know I thought it first

Parted Souls

Find the man,
Who killed his daughter.
Trial or search,
No one bothered.

Found the man,
That got off free.
He struck him once,
Then fell to his knees.

With no more strength,
He cried and wept.
The man killed him too,
With no regrets.

You took his soul,
When you killed his girl.
But they're 2gether again,
In another world.

And Yet I Still Want You . . .

Rejection after rejection,
I jettison the pain from peers
Change my appearance
In hopes to appear in the light
I know I got the lightning presence
Yet I have yet to hear my name behind "(blank) Presents"
Cause another rejection
Makes me feel like a reject
Learn dialect after dialect
To follow directing
My abilities constantly they're dissecting
And my sanity they continue testing
I've felt near hopeless I can attest
Another trial another test,
Just to hear thanks for coming in
But I'll never give up
Cause even though, you say no now
I'm getting closer
I will get there
No matter the pain you put me through
Cause . . . No matter what,
I still want you . . .

Enter the Black Hole

It's in another universe
Brings you to another dimension
Contents completely unknown
Destination guesses are hypothetical
The guess is infinite space
Mystical and mysterious
So don't get inside my thoughts
You may never get out

6 Feet Deep

```
===========================
===========================
===========================
   _____
  /time with &@&$%----------------|
 / |accomplishments and failures---|
|  |times I was silent or not silent---|
| / \my chosen mistakes-------------|
 \_/_____/
```

Is it Any Better Up There (4-2Pac)

Judge me now
Judge me over and over again
I write what I want
And if I want too I'll write it again
Judge my words
It's different than the last poem I wrote
You say "He contradicted himself in the same book"
But, I'll contradict myself in the same poem
You reckon I have no beliefs
You deem my visions impaired
But maybe it's me writing both views?
Yet you don't believe that's true
Can I not change my opinion too?
Maybe I'm not the problem
Maybe the problem . . . is with you . . .

She Waits... For His Return

She Waits, Jittery
    4 His Return
She Asks 4 My Admirable Advice
    4 I Have Helped Others
        Yet She Knows She's Incapable of Taking It
She Knows He's No Good 4 Her
    And No Matter How Many Times I Remind Her
        She Waits 4 His Return
She Says She Thinks She's Going To Die of Love For Him
    Sadly Eventually She'll Be Right
She Knows He's Had Many Others
    And She's Heard The Stories, 4
        He Did Them All Wrong, Yet
She Waits 4 His Return
She Waits 4 His Return
    Even Though She Knows
        -Others Have Never Recovered
            -From The Drama He Creates
She's Heard The Ending 2 Each Story
    Kadee Got Pregnant Because of Him
        And Because of Him She Doesn't Even Know
            -Who The Father Is
    It Gets Worse Cause Azure's Family
        -Turned Their Back On Her
    Jordan? I Heard She's No Longer With Us
    Jenny She Just It's Been
        -Awhile Since Her Name Was Even Heard of
    Ree-Ree She's Gone Too
        They Just Haven't Buried Her Yet
    But Stephanie I Heard She's Doing Fine
        Well I Mean She Lost Everything
        And She Still Has Nightmares
            Scared She'll Relapse and Go Back To Him
            Psychologically Still In Pain
                But She's Lucky She's Still Here
                And Can At Least Feel Pain
                Real Pain

> Not His Pain
> All The While

She Waits 4 His Return
> No Matter What I Say She Won't Listen
>> Funny What You Will or Won't Do When
>>> -Your In Love

She Just Waits 4 His Return
> Eventually She'll Realize How Wrong He Is
>> When Loves Involved Sometimes You Have To
>>> -Find Out For Yourself
>> But I'm Afraid By Then It Will
>>> -Be 2 Late . . . For Her

She Doesn't Realize What He's Already Done To Her
So She Waits 4 His Return
She Can't See How He's Changed Her . . . For The Worse
She Loves Him Too Much
And One Night That's Exactly What Happened
As She Walked Back To The Mutual
> -Friend That Introduced Them

And Explained How Long It's Been Since
> -She's Seen Him

They Both Did Not Know It Would Be Her
> -Last Visit

But Like The Second Time And Every
> -Visit After That

She Did It So Poetically
> As She Said
>> *"I've Been Waiting*
>> *Waiting 4 U To Take Me Again*
>> *What U Do 2 Me I Can't Explain*
>> *We Should Never Be Apart This Long . . .*
>> *So Return*
>> *Return Often And Save Me*
>> *Desire, and Lust Return And Save Me*
>> *Take Me With You My Love,*
>> *Take Me Often*
>> *I Know You're In My Heart*
>>> *Cause You Run Through My Veins,*
>> *Just Touch My Skin, And I'll Remember*

Take Me Once Again
For Then I'll Get My Wings Back
      And Feel, As If I Can Fly Again,
Literally . . .
Take Me With You—My Love Is 4 U
My Life Is Yours"

So On That Night
She Had Waited 4 Him 4 Sooo Long
She Longed 4 His Companionship Sooo Much
That She Had Grown To Love Him Too Much
So On That Night She Took More Love From Him
      Than She Could handle
She Loved Him So Much She Started 2 Bleed
      No Not Down There
She Bled From Her Arm
She Didn't Use Handcuffs or Ropes With Him
      Well Sometimes Ropes but Most of The
          -Time It Was A Leather Belt
She Uses them not for Restrain
      But Rather To Find her Veins
Substituting Pain For Pain
      His Pain
U Wanna Know His Name
They Call Him New Millennium Smack
Hot Azz Liquid Heroine Laced w/ Cocaine

Radio

You Wanna Play With The Radio
Don't Play With The Radio
So You Press Play On The Radio
Just Wanting To Use A Sample
But Now The Beat Has You Addicted
And Makes You Press Rewind
And Turn Up The Volume
Take Some More Of The Volume
Take Some More Volume
Take More Valume
Now The Volume Throws Your Balance Off
And The Treble Makes You Tremble
Looking For A Reprise
Jonzin For A New Single
While Your Stuck On Pause
You Scrape Up Some Change
For the Jukebox
Repeat And Repeat Again
Repeat & Then Stop . . .
But The Music Starts Up Again
No Longer Censored
Containing Explicit Content
To Make Enough To Get Airplay
And All You Can Think About Is Fast-Forwarding
      To Another Hit
But Your Skipping, Skipping, Skipping
All Scratched Up
But You Want To Hear The
Comforting Crackle
As You Let Go Of The Needle
Record & Re-Record & Re-Record
Until You Got A Playlist
And The Compilations Your Record
Sing The Refrain, That You've Been Reframed
Bootlegging, Copying, You're On Tape
Behind 16 Bars Looking For A New Release Date

You Try To Shuffle It Up
But It Goes Back To Your Classic Song
Press Skip, Same Song, But New Artist Sings The Cover
Remixed From A Mix-Tape
Featuring A Guest Appearance You Can't Take
Lyrics Misinterpreted
Now The Cracklings Clear
The Cracklings Clear
Last Hook Goes Through
The Receiver Loud . . . Deaf
The Bass Makes The Head Shake . . . Deaf
More Bass & The Head Shakes Deaf
More Bass, Head Shakes Deaf
Bass-Head Shakes . . . Death

giving you a chance . . . (a daughters gift)

Mom Tells Me All About U
And There's So Many Things, That I Wish That U Knew
Sometimes Just Someone 2 Talk 2
But You're Always Gone, "Doing What U Do"

Never Knew My First Words,
      Or Seen My First Steps
Forgiven,
Cause I Don't Remember Either,
But Hope You're Here For What's Next

Back Briefly,
      But Gone Again For My First Day Of School
Sent Home Sick The First Week,
      Not From Illness, I Just Really Miss You

I Know In My Heart, Someday You'll Be Around
I Dream About That Day As You Light Up Everything Around
I 4Give U Cause You're My Dad, My Idle
And It's Why I 4Gave U 4 Being "Out"
      On The Night Of My First Violin Recital

And Yesterday U Came To My 4th Grade Class
Picked Me Up In The Air + Said "We're Going To The Mall Honey!"
We Stopped At The Corner Store, As You Bumped
Into A Friend, & Argued Over 'Owing Money'

You Both Proceeded To Argue And Push,
      As Both Your Eyes, Filled Slowly With Hate And Geed
I Begged You To Come,
      As I Tugged On Your Sleeve
You Lightly Pushed Me Away,
      & Told Me "This Grown Man Business"
Not Old Enough To Understand Why You Won't Leave With Me,
      But Old Enough 2 Know, This Is Something I Don't Wanna Witness
He Pulled Out A Gun And Pointed It In Your Face
      I Screamed, You Lunged, He Shot,

And Three Shots Sprayed . . .
U Were Never There For Me
    But I Was Here For You Today
Cause The Bullet Was Meant For You
    But I Took It, In Your Place
U Lived Life As If With No Daughter
Therefore I Lived My Life, Like I Had No Father
Your Conscious Would Say . . .
"Look At Those Innocent Eyes"
    Instead U Would Leave & Go
Conscious Would Say . . .
"Look Into Those Innocent Eyes"
    & Then U Would Go
Conscious Says Now . . .
"Last Chance 2 C Those Innocent Eyes . . . B4 They Close"
U Seen Them B4, But Will U Remember?
U Saw Them B4, Way Back, Last December
So I Finished My Life With No Father
Now You Can Continue Finishing Yours
    Same As Always
        With No Daughter . . .

Amnesia 1wonone

Ne proumiavam
不知所措
छवियाँ
giọng nói
ومضـات

jetzt noch immer ohne Anhaltspunkt . . .
I don't know
Qui je suis
¿Quién soy yo?

to2 Amnesia twotoo

Te gen yon aksidan—
Σκέφτομαι
NE SJECAM SE NICEGA.
Waar I ben
Кто ты?
Que paso?

Tres Amnesia Three . . . 3

i only know. i am me ... yet couldn't give you a name
i know everything. yet can't name it. and don't know why.
What year would i start at. For guessing?
Look at everything ... surrounded by too many details
the reason would be the easiest guess
the voice said ..." because"

For Amnesiã 4Foür

我只知道，我是我 . . . 但不能給你一個名字

أنـا أعرف كـل شـي, عـلـى الـرغم مـن ذلـك لا اسـتطيع تسـميته, و لا أعرف لمـاذا

In welchem Jahr würde ich mit dem Schätzen anfangen?
mira todo—rodeado por demasiodos detalles
Причиной было бы самое простое предположение
eu mok so ri neun "we" nya g

Notes From Heaven

Someday I'll B with U
Do U know the other part of U

When I'm missing U
I'm missing half of me
I'm missing U
Because U should B next 2 me You're a part of me

If U C me don't B scared of Me
      Come 2 me Cause You're a part of me
For 6 years I've saved a Kiss 4 U

Chapter 5

Songs

Are songs poetry? I would have said no, at one point in time. But how can it not be? Not all poems are songs, and not all songs are poetry. But how can one not say that Bill Withers, Stevie Wonder, Bob Dylan, Erykah Badu or Tupac Shakur doesn't sing their poetry? The same way you can't say that Shakespeare or Langston Hughes doesn't make you sing their words.

Filled with Tearz

It's almost been a year
Still my eyes are filled with tearz
And now when I look in the mirror
You're no longer here
Even though we are apart
I swear I can feel your heart
I thought I needed a cure
But all I need is you . . .
To be here
And take away my tearz

Refrain 1: We always said forever
But we're no longer together
And to take away my misery
You gotta come back to me
Our promise is now a lie
I already lost my mind
So I'm asking you baby
Will you come walk with me
Cause I swear that I am sorry

We had a rough year I know
So you felt you had to go
Suddenly you disappeared
How can you be far away
When your spirits still right here
Now I'm waiting for the day
When you'll say you'll come back home
But many months have dawned
And my heart is still alone
Everyone said you're gone
But I'm still waiting for you
Cause I know our love was true

Refrain 2: We always said forever
But we're no longer together

And to take away my misery
You gotta come back to me
All because of a lie
Our promise is now a crime
I'm going out of my mind
So I'm asking you baby
Will you come walk with me
Cause I swear that I am sorry

One quiet night
Something just wasn't right
And I just broke down and died
Cause I swore I heard you cry
I could hear your thoughts
I swear I heard you talk
I couldn't sleep that night
Cause you were my light
Now I'm on my knees
Begging you baby please
Come back to me
And I'll never lie to you again
You are my love
And you were my friend
We're supposed to be together
All the way to the end

<u>Refrain 1</u>
<u>Refrain 2</u>
Refrain 1

Do "you" Love Me

When I look into your eyes
        I can see the lies you made
You can look to the future
        but you can't change yesterday

Each time I see you
        the lovin still remains
But it's hard to keep on moving
        when our feelings aren't the same

Been apart a long long time but at night
        my hearts in pain

But feelings always stay and feelings always
change and no one really knows what they mean
it's all a dream

If we work it all out and work it all through
        I'd be in my bed
                right next to you oh you

So if you really love me
then please don't play no games
Or my heart will end up broken
        from enduring too much pain

I know it's hard to love with a broken
Heart
        And it's impossible to say I Love you
But if you can heel your broken heart

    I'll be back to love you

When it's cold inside
    and my bodies full of pain
I know that you will comfort me
    even if our feelings changed

So never mind the past
    cause nothing stays the same
So tell me if you love me
    it's all that's left to say

My Release Part 1

Have Some 1 Tip U 2 The Real Side
Trying To Deceive Not Manipulation Made My Soul Die
Some Place Between Your Story And Hers
Is Where "Your Truth" Lies

I Know Drama Made Things Change In A Rush
So Much We Seemed Out Of Touch
Avalanches, Lost & Confused It Got Rough
Stand-Up I'm Your Support Not Your Crutch

No Time For Games I've Already Played
Look Up, But U Need 2 Find Your Own Trade
Make Mistakes Constantly, Carefully
But B Careful Of What U've Made

Nightmares No Longer Just Imagination
Disgusted, U Don't Even See It As A Temptation
Temporary Illusions Seeking Validation
/Slash/ A Simple Minded Way Of Escaping

Short-Lived Gratification, Fabricated Truth Of What U C
Momentary Fulfillment Of What U Think U Need
Blow It Out, Exhale, Release The Fury & The Greed
Pain Can B Brief If U Learn 2 Breathe

But You Don't Really Need Me,
2 C Your Actions Can Only Make Yourself Bleed
Time Is On Your Side If It's What U Need
Careful, It Will Only B With U Temporarily

My Release Part 2

Everything I Had, U Consumed With Your Greed
U Sucked Every Last Drop I Could Bleed
Now It's Time For U 2 C Your Sad Reality
Your Nothing Like Me & That's Y U Despise Me

Perception Is Tainted Blurry As It Pours
Ironically, That's All U Ever Cared For
Truth Is Deep, But U Seem 2 B Closer 2 The Shore
U & Me, Eye 2 Eye, Is Something Never More

I'm Not Above Anyone But I'm Above U
Sounds Wrong 2 Say But Sadly It Became True
Others Thoughts, (huh) If They Only Knew
I Just Hope The Next Person Runs Away From U . . .

Frustration Built From Everything You've Done
Bad Memories Outweigh The Good 4 To 1
In Conclusion It's Time 2 Release The Past
With That Said U & Me R Done.

The next group of poems are called . . . *Fantasy Poems*. I must explain for you to understand. They are compact, because that's how dreams are. A good dream, that always ends too soon. I got the idea for these when I fell asleep on the beach, and quickly dreamt of a beautiful girl talking to me from this exotic place. However, I was awoken by a wave. Although I awoke to soon to finish the dream, it was just in time to see a girl pass by, who looked very similar to the one I had just dreamt about. Whether or not I had seen her before gave me an idea. Maybe exotic fantasies are dressed in plain clothes all around us. We just don't know. So in each fantasy I see a different girl in one way, only to be awakened by her reality.

Nyurican Fantasy

Nyurican Butta Pecan Pure Bronx
Puerto Rican, Know she's got me as she softly
calls out *"Hey Papi"* Thinking 'look at
what Destiny brought me' Not long
passes till she all my Mami and sighing
"¡Aye Papi!" As she Tops me Rocks me
And Then Cold water shocks me.

COLUMBIAN FANTASY

Walking in the Mountains, I see her stare
like an angel as if
appearing from nowhere, as the breeze
blows her hair with her scent stealing
the fresh airs Traditionally dressed smile
makes the rest look like less listen to whatever
She says Convo keeps me even more awake
than her cousin Juan Valdez

Bahamian Fantasy

On the beach in beautiful Barbados
Then she walks by like a tornado,
powerful but graceful demanding attention
with each step and stride speaks to me
I glide feel like I'm walking on Air Talking
to someone Identical to Aaliyah then she
lips "I need ya" As I Unwantingly Leave Ya

TRINIDADIAN FANTASY

Eyez meet eyez only thing I can see
besides stomach and thighs with your
costume grabbing the attention
I knew you were 4 me
without question After the Festival wanted
to get to know the best of you went dinin',
then just chillin + limin and then
grindin + grindin + grindin Before you were
wearing 20 lbs of thread at The Carnival
Now Your Removing Every Article But
My time runs out B4 I touch every part of you

Mexican Fantasy

Goddesses
everywhere you look in every single
angle But you stood out in the city of angels
making hearts ache with your long curly hair
chins drop + you take away their air
as you talked spanglish while you stroked mine
you made my body shake
more than a 4.8 earthquake
(then) you give me aftershocks
too bad It doesn't last cause I heard the door
knock

Unknown Fantasy

Far away from home I met you on
the beach all alone immediately hung up
your phone "I'll call you back" And You
were the one spittin like a Mack Mami w/
control No games so Let the love making commence
as the ride hits turbulence but this is only
a sample of something great can't stay
I'm finally at the gate

Peruvian Fantasy

Anissa The Diva From Lima Freak of Nature
like LA Nina Top Notch Butterscotch Baby got Butters
and gets you crunk like scotch
backs
up the solo chichera talk and lets you watch
Got the girls of your dreams in Peru Found out
Treschera talk is true We Both say
"I do" But then I roll in the pool

Cuban Fantasy

Beach to Beach Beautiful Women
but They still ain't you In the City of
fake breasts you fake-less inspiration of
what women wannabe envied by everybody
so bad Like
a role 'model' they look at and say "that's
what I'm gonnabe" To the point of surgery
Needless to say I'm flattered that
You want me Caliente Cuban Mami "De
donde" 'Miami' Now It must be 3 cause
you alarm me

Unfortunately for us, our eulogies will be written by people other than ourselves. They will write something that will make us sound much better than we actually were. However each exaggeration will based on a truth. So here's the opposite side to even things out. A pre-eulogy if you will. Something to make me sound worse than I was, but also based on some truth . . .

My Eulogy

Questions we raised from thoughts
Styles made so hot,
Take what he got
He caught sleepin' no creepin'
Daylight skeamin' is reality
No need embellishing
Moments relished in like these
Stay live in the streets
In the streets we pass
'Cause got more ground than that
Work every county, hide U 4 "bounty"
Til we turned cars @ 13
So when U sleep
U C me doing everything U dream
After small hits, systems legit
Pour your soul out 4 me
I bleed out 4 U, True
I'll pour this liquor 4 U
Cause you're about 2 tip your glass
4 a thirsty past following me
I'm runnin' on E
Saying it's time 4 me
Don't B blue just
Watch the news &
Pour out some 4 me 2

—He was survived by, anyone who truly met him and knew him.

Chapter 6

THE STORM . . .

I named this section the storm cause even the dark side has some light to it. The light may hurt, but it's still light. I truly had a hard time seeing it, but it was there.

Witness the Storm.

𝒴? Can't 👁 …❓"Dream

👁 know 👁 can't Dream❓
    That is Evident

The ?Question? is Y

Is There A **Deeper** Meaning /////Behind
    My Inability 2 Breathe at Night ☞

Or Do 👁   Just Have 2 Much 2 Much 2 Much 2 Much 2 Much
        Clouding
        My Mind

𝒴? Can 👁 Not 𝒟𝑅𝐸𝒜𝑀

Yes At Night☞ My 👁'z R Closed
    But That Is No Reason 4
    Me, 2 Not B ABLE 2 C . . .

Maybe My Mind Is ⇉Stuck⇇
Or Maybe 👁 𝒟𝑅𝐸𝒜𝑀 Things So
    Beautiful Only 2 Wake Up The Next
    Morning Penny-less 4 The Night ☞

| Maybe 👁 Feel There's Nothing 2 Dream |
| About . . . |

If So
> Give Me A Reason 2 Dream

It's Not That 👁 Don't Want 2
> 👁 Can't

Maybe in the Back of My Mind
> Or Deep Inside 👁've Given Up
>> Hope

My Mind But Not My Heart . . .
> If That's The Problem That Is

Point is . . .
👁 Can't Dream
👁 Don't Know 𝒴
Maybe U Can Help
𝒴? Can't 👁 . . . ?'"𝒟𝑅ℰ𝒜ℳ

My Time Is Almost Up

In Time It Will All Explode
My Time That Is
While Ya'll Try And Cut My Wires
U Caution Unsure Why
Afraid People Will Die + Others Disoriented
True In A Way
Some Close 2 Me Will Die In Their Hearts
Ones I've Touched Will B Drained 2 No Life
I Believe All Will Move On
However They'll 4Ever B Disoriented
Wondering Why?
Never Understanding Why Things Happened
The Way They Did
They Know It Should Never Have Ended Like This
And U're 2 Blame
Scared Of Me
    Or Threatened
But Why . . . ?
Cause U Chose Not 2 Know Me
Whether Time Ends With No Drama
    Disappear In The Night
Wires R Cut—We Both Lose
    4-Ever Trapped
Or It Ends In The Vision I C
    In An Explosion
    But An Explosion on Me
That Is What I Feel
That Is What I C
I'm Sure,
In Time, It Will All Explode
Victimized Because U Chose
Only What U Wanted 2 C

When Will My Past Catch Up?

My Heart Beats Faster
I can Feel It Coming
How much Will Make It?
👁 Don't know . . .

It Makes Me Cry
But So Does My Present
But Will I Cry In the Future.?
   —If My Present Meets My Past—
      I Only Worry Cause My Past Is Coming . . . Coming

👁 Now Look 2 The Future
Cause The Bad in The Past,
      Is in the Past
Though The Past Will Never Last
Its Still Yet 2 B Gone

If It Catches Me
I'll B OK
I Will Survive
   My Past Is Coming
I Will Live . . .
   Unless It's That
      And Then 👁 Die . . .

It's Coming . . . Coming . . . Coming . . . Coming

My Past Is Coming

Visions of a dark day
When the sun turns gray
Only days away
Yet 👁 have only minutes left

White t-shirt turned red
Aneurisms 4 my head
Soon 2 B dead
It's different each time

Not just dreams
If 👁 bled 👁 bleed
Takes my breath 👁 breathe
So how can 👁 re-write it?

Just Give Me The Answer

Eyes tell all
Eyes show pain
Don't ask what's wrong
Don't ask if I'm ok
Don't point out the obvious
It's obvious what's ever so real
My eyes will tell you the truth
My eyes will ask the question
Don't ask me "What can I do?"
Don't give me words of hope
Just give me the answer, or
walk on by . . .

Do Not Wake Me When Eye Dream —It's All I Have Left

I got somewhere to be at 8:00am
My alarm is set for 7:00
Let the alarm clock do its job
Don't wake me before
Don't call me to tell me your news
Just wait
Wait until I'm already awake
If I'm tossing and turning
Let me go until I fall off the bed.
Bed hahaha I mean couch
Or the floor
And since I can't fall off that
Let me sleep it's a dream it's all I have left
You ask, "What if you're screaming in your sleep?"
A nightmare? "Yeah"
Let me sleep
Do not wake me
Let me sleep
I do not want to be waken cause
I know
At least the dream isn't real . . .

I Hate You

You ask how I can be filled with hate.
Look at you.
You're the poster child for disappointment.
Promises of bright lights and fame . . .
Promises of teachings to the brain . . .
You ask how can I hate?
How can I not when I look at you?
You forget I'm on your side.
I'm just saying your letting everyone down.
Everyone that's ever known you . . .
The ones who lost to you, lost to this?
The ones who beat you, excelled because you set the bar?
Who's going to push them now?
Stop being scared.
You say you do best with pressure on you . . .
Well here you go.
I'm looking you directly in the eye, and asking you . . .
How can such a beautiful reflection,
Paint such an ugly picture?

Is It My Destiny (2 B Lonely)

Someone told me a scientific theory,
That life is a loop.
Life being the complete cycle of life
From reincarnation, or the
Life energy, or your essence to the next . . .
As it transforms in your next host
The theory says that you will
Continue to do the same things in this life
That you did in your previous one and so on.
Make the same decisions and mistakes
If were talking about this time itself
The loneliness would make sense in my life . . . now.
If this is going to continue on
For lives and lives to come . . .
Does that mean, for eternity,
I will see this again and again?
Is it my destiny to be lonely?

DEAD SOUL WALKING 1 & 2

Take Your Hand off My Shoulder
I Can't Feel It Anyway
So Close 2 My Heart
But Souls Gone Far Away

Sand Hits My Face +
Smoke Clouds my way
20-20 Blurred As U
Wear White 2 My Grave

Can't Hear U Talkin (cause)
I'm A Dead Soul Walking

We Shared The Suns Rays & + Drank The Clouds Rain
Day After Day After Day After Day After Day After Day
Til The Day Turned Grey
I'm A Dead Soul

Didn't C U Leave
Cause U were still In Front of Me
My Soul Still Breathes
But soon 2 B Taken away
away, away from me
Walking to my last prayer
Blind me with a glare
Can't act like I don't care
U can C it in my eyes
Heart beat on the rise
Taking away something money can't buy
Even Through Everything
No Peace When the Angels sing (cause I)
just want to hear it ring

Dead Soul Walking 1.5

Open the cell
My final visitation
Done surgically w/no hesitation
Hope turns to frustration
Last Comfort
Doesn't Comfort Anymore
Gotta Drug me too/through
As I hit the floor
Don't Take my Air
(Gotta Keep Walkin') N walkin
Dead Soul Walkin

The Rain, The Storm

10 million miles away
The sun shows the way
If I wanna live past Today

A Better future is near
Unfortunately I gotta start here
this year bleeding tears

taking my first steps
I wish I had my shoes
but U gotta bleed to sing the blues

2 heal my wounds
I gotta feel yours
Add on the weight as it rains
to increase the Red shores

They say I walk Against the Grain
But By Now my feet can take the pain

Many revelations made
Along the way
What I thought would Be Strong or Evergreen
Found they needed to leave

The Oak + pine couldn't handle the limited
Give + take like the tropicals + me
Can't show any fear here

They wait 4 the weakness to live +

Nothing new is found on the bridge

From wading to the deep is
Where I found my skeleton key
Drying from Desert Heat
The Predators begin 2 follow me

small drink left from chipped english Tea
But this + that is all I need
U can stalk me, charge me + follow me but your not
gonna swallow me

Where I'm going to is just as important
As where I've gone
I'm here at last as
The Wall was a mirage all along

>   —dedicated to Mrs. Marks a teacher that most students
> can only hope for . . .

WHITE LADY

I Need 2 Escape
But You're Not The One
    "Come With Me
      I'll Show You What needs 2 B Done"
U Tried This Before
And It Didn't Work Then
    "Freaking Out
      When U Know U Wanna Get Bent"
I Never Needed U Before
+ Don't Need U Now
    "U Always Needed This But
     Never More Than U Do Right Now"
U Stalking Me When I'm Happy
+ Still There Things Are Going Downhill
    "Taking This Roller-Coaster +
     I'll Show U How good U can Feel
     U Know How Much People Desire Me
     I F*ck Them So Good They Can't Breathe
     👁's Can't C Pain's Cold Reality"
That Ain't 4 Me
    "But U can cut me, Sell Me
     + Tell Me Your OK C'ing Everyone Else w/Me?
     Just Grit Your Teeth, Breathe Deep +
     Put Your Tongue On Me
     I'll Make It better Than Your Mind Can Dream"
That Was a Temporary 'Friendship'
2 Many Close Calls With U IN My Grip
Now I Know U Ain't 4 Me
I Knew U Was Never 4 Me
Just Glad I Flipped U When I Did
    "Taste Me"
Never
    "U Can Leave"
I Will
    "But U Know This Isn't It"
Yeah!? 2 Bad It Is
This Secrets Gonna Die With Me
    "No You're Going Down With Me"

Chapter 7

. . . After The Storm

A lot of stuff was still needed to be cleaned up, but that's an always type thing. I'm cleaning things up one by one, so I won't have to deal with them again. You get solace from knowing other people have gone through what you have. You also get comfort, that when the storm is over, you can change the things you worry about. If you can't change them why worry?

Is It My Destiny (2 B Lonely) Part Deuce

Lonely . . .
For a lifetime? No
I never was . . .
Many have come and gone
But they were here.
Hard to see,
When you're looking for something lasting
But I've never been left alone
And If I have to do it all again,
I'll be happy to see your faces once more
Friends have came and went,
And you all left to soon
But you were here when I needed you most
And for that, I may be lonely,
But I was never alone . . .

When 👁 Rest, 👁 Now Rest in Peace . . . (So Please Let Me Sleep)

When 👁 Rest,
    It is true,
        That 👁 No Longer Dream
            But 👁 No Longer Dream of Death
                      Either

    Nightmares are gone
        Insomnia No longer a factor
And Though 👁 No Longer Dream
    👁 can Sleep—And 👁 do
    No Dreams but No Nightmares

👁 No Longer Dread My eyelids getting Heavy
And No Longer Fear what 👁,
    Will C, Again,
        When They Close

When 👁 Rest 👁 May Not B Dreaming.
    But 👁'm Sleeping in Peace
        Finally
              . . . finally
    so please let me sleep

U ease my soul   dedicated to T.M.

U ease my soul
    Just Knowing you're there
        Makes my heart beat
            It beats slow no doubt,
                But it beats

U ease my soul
    Thinking that 👁 might C U 2morrow
        Every Time 👁 step outside
            👁 understand, might be the moment
                I C U

It eases my soul
    When I dream of what might B 2 Come,
        Whether I already Know U
            Seen U once,
                Yet 2 meet,
                      Or Are Already Staring Me
                          in the Eyez

Just Knowing That
    When 👁 Truly C U
        U'll B Perfect In My Eyez
            Just Knowing That Somewhere
                You're Out There . . .

                        . . . U ease my soul . . .

Just Dream—4 Me

You No Longer Stand Next 2 Me
And U No Longer Lay Next 2 Me
And Though You're No Longer By My Side
All 👁 Have 2 Do When I Wanna C Your eyez
    Is Dream
        Just Dream . . .
  Dream
        When I Miss U, 👁 Dream
          Just Dream
Dream, Dream, Dream
When 👁 feel Blue
👁 Dream
We Used 2 Chill + Burn Money
All Day Til We Got Hungry
I Fed U, U Fed Me
You're Gone But Instead Of Reminiscing
I Can Chill With U 4 Real
👁 Just Got 2 Dream
Dream and Dream Again
When 👁 Need U I Dream
  Dream
            Dream
    Dream
      👁 . . . Dream
I Miss U Almost Every Second I'm Awake
But When It Hurts 👁 Close My I's
And When My Heart Needs U Eye Dream
When 👁 Want U 👁 Dream
  Just Dream
    Dream
      Dream
        Dream

Thanks 2 My Scars

The blood was thick
But they told it could B stopped
The wounds ran deep
They told me they could B healed
The scars came thick
They told me they would stay

Each cut & gash
Would leave marks 2 last
Blemishes they R not
The scars R mine
The scars R me

👁 love each one
They remind of what was
They remind me of what is
They help distinguish reality from delusion
Reality is the scars
It reminds me the past is real

It's Not So Bad, It's Not So Bad

Back then 👁 took a picture now
👁 took a picture back then
The picture was 4 now
In-case 👁 felt like-I-did back then
Frustration builds up
Things R more than dim
When things feel stuck . . ." F*ck!"
👁 look back, @ way back then
Fact is things R always bad
No matter what U have
But pictures of the low points
Remind me it's not so bad
It's not so bad
From where I came
2 where I am
It's not so bad
It's not so bad . . .

I Saw U Behind Me In The Mirror—Dedicated 2 Hope

I saw U the other day
i saw U standing there
U follow me
U follow me often
True you're not always there
But your visits R more frequent
Coincidently my spirit is
Raise me up
I'm no longer down when you're not around
Cause the fact your coming around
Makes me smile and bounce my head
      Like a good song
The reflection behind me in the mirror isn't me
But it's getting closer ☺

Do Not Wake Me 👁 May B Free

👁 don't know what happened
👁 didn't give up 👁 know that
But 👁 feel peace
But nothing was solved
I'm not so tired that 👁 don't care anymore
I'm not happy with where things are going
I'm not satisfied
Not, no longer scared
Nothing has changed but time
And time doesn't heal all scars
It helps but you need more than time to heal
Don't believe me, see these wounds
Still pain
Everything almost exactly the same
👁 don't know what happened
But a small sense of peace has reached me
Still uneasy when awake
But 👁 can sleep
👁 may finally be free
Eyes closed peacefully
Peace will come soon when they're open too.
But Do Not Wake Me . . .
👁 May Be Free . . .

Sometimes 👁 Cry

Sometimes I cry
Not from pain
Physical or Mental

Sometimes I cry
Not because I'm Scared,
Afraid or Nervous

Sometimes I Cry
Not because I'm Happy
Or overjoyed with Excitement

Sometimes I cry
Not from sadness
Or Dismay

Sometimes I cry
Not from being proud
Or Embarrassed

Sometimes I cry
Cause of where we came
& that we made it through

Sometimes I cry,
When I look back
And I don't know why

Chapter 8

Thoughts of Love

Of course Love poems are the most common favorite. But I don't know what a Love poem is, and every time I think I do it changes. It's Thoughts of Love. From when you think you might be falling, to when you realize you might be, or you were in Love. You never truly know when Love strikes, or how hard it will hit you. Thoughts of Love means anytime you think that Love could be creeping up on you, or that you are, but you're not willing to admit yet. It also is when you wish you hadn't been in Love, or when you thought you were, but you weren't.

Maybe . . . ?

Maybe When We Met . . .
The Reason We Thought We Already Knew Each Other, Was
Cause We Were Together In Another Life
Maybe The Reason We Got So Close, Was 2 Help
Each Other Through The Struggle & Strife

Maybe We R Soul Mates Because We Were The
Same Person At One Time
Maybe We Became Best Friends Cause Of The
Passion We Hold 4 Each Others Mind

Maybe We're Not Enemies Cause We Believe In
Each Other But Trust 4 Others Is Poor
Maybe We're Allies Cause We're Fighting Similar
Wars

Maybe You're My Future Or Soon 2 B Just My Past
Maybe The Reason We're Not Lovers Is Cause There's
More 2 Us Than Just That

Maybe You're A Tease, Cause U Leave When I
Couldn't Possibly Love U N-E-MORE
Maybe U Own My Heart Cause When U Come Back
I Fall Deeper Than I Did Before

Maybe You're My Angel Cause U Alwayz Change
My Life Each Time You're Here
Maybe You're My Demon Cause I'm Fine Until U Reappear

Maybe I Love U and 4-ever 2getherness is
      Our Fate
Maybe I Hate U Cause U Need Time And
Your Making Me Wait

Maybe You're My Light That Burns Strong With
Truth
Maybe My Heart Hurts Cause It Was Filled By U

Maybe You're My Drug Cause I Feel I Need U But
I Don't
Maybe You're My Antidote That Let's Me
Float

Maybe You're My Dream Where I Wish 2 Sleep
4-Ever But Can't
Maybe You're My Nightmare That I Try 2 Run From
But I Stand

Maybe You're My Passion That With Each Minute
Gets Stronger & Stronger
Maybe It's U That Gives Me This Pain I Can't
Take Much Longer

Maybe The Reason We're Not One Is Cause Our Time
Has Yet 2 Come
Maybe The Reason U Ripped Out My Heart Is Because
U Didn't Have One

2 B Continued . . .

Maybe . . . (Continued & Finished)

**Maybe The Reason I Hate U So Much
Is Because I Can't Stop Loving U . . .**

One More Night ☪

Conversations With Our Eyes
Moments With Our Hearts
Hold Me Close And We Touch Souls
I Need One More Night
Conversations From A Glance
Body Language Speaks With Desire
I Can Feel Your Heart Beating On Me
I Need One More Night
Smiles Make Hearts Beat
Hugs Make Knees Weak
A Touch Lasts 4 Ever
That's Why I Need One More Night
Excitement At Sight Creates Inner Smiles
Lips That Kiss Makes Pain Worthwhile
Nights Will Never Be 4Gotten
So Give Me One More Night
And My Soul Can Rest 4 Ever

These poems are written in the Hmong language. I do not speak Hmong but I worked really hard writing a short poem and then looking up every single word and translating it from a book. What I had hoped for was for it to make sense but sound better in Hmong since translation is never exact. The second one is slightly altered after having a Hmong person translate and tell me what it meant. So you have the rough poem and the revised versions.

Love!

Kuv muaj ib yaam twg saab huv
      Kev paub kuv ua tau tsi yog
           Tsi yob, tab sis tsi yog
Taag nrho kuv tau muaj peer xwm ua
    —nyob sau nwg nqeg rua hauv qaab

Love?

Kuv muaj ib yaam twg saab huv
      Tsis yog lawm, tab sis ho yog
Taag nrho kuv muaj peev xwm ua
    —nyob sau rua hauv qaab

Where The Red Fern Grows

I made your Eulogy and recited it twice
👁 stand with your grave everyday, in
      my ♥ that is
In it's place A Red Fern Grows
Red is The Hate that replaced the love
      cause 👁 really can't give it 2 another
Green is the envy I feel. As 👁 sit here
      miserable you're living your life
A Red Fern grows in the place U used
      2 B
The Place U came and The Place 👁
      buried U
Unless A Miracle comes My Heart will
      Die
It Will Starve As it sits in pain
      Suffering from Starvation

                Dedicated 2 Kari

If U Should Die —4 Theresa

I am What 👁 am B-cause of U
I have grown and overcome cause of
    the food U made
I have hope and B-lief B-cause of the
    love U've Given
But Yet I only feel contempt B-Cause
    of the light I've put in your eyes
I feel Ashamed B-Cause of your
    B-lief in my skillz
I weep in my heart B-Cause of where
    U B-lieve 👁 will go + where I am at
Happy 👁 am not or may 👁 ever B
Though when I hear U speak 👁 no longer
    want 2 cry
4 If U were no longer here what would happen
    with me:
No one 2 help me fix the mistakes I've
    made
Or More importantly stop me from committing
    2 more
No advice or late night phone calls 2 ease
    my soul
In moments of selfishness I hope 2 Die B4
    U So I don't feel That Pain
But If U Die Take me with . . .
If my Angel leaves I will cry and
    may drown in my own tearz
If U Die 👁 shall Die with U cause
    no one could understand
If U should leave no one call, I
    will know
The Heart she built like everything
    else will fall back down
(Back 2 my oak) 👁 may survive
    in your absence
But no matter How Lucky I may B
If U Should Die, 👁 *WILL BLEAD*

My lil Secret —2 N.D.

👁 judge ever girl I meet
Based on a standard set by you
You're everything a woman should be
From head to toe, and everything inside
Intelligence, class and beauty
When you pass guys
You make them exhale
Little do they know
Your all they see and more
Every guy that's known you has
Probably felt way more than just friendship,
As did I
I'm Sorry I never told you
But your so . . .
Well, you make it hard to tell you
My lil Secret
That you're everything I've wanted
And more . . .

Childhood Sweetheart

Talking on the phone all night
Going 2 the county fair
Riding bikes across the city 2 C each other
Stopping by your work 2 C U
Making out @ the YMCA
Making plans 2 C a movie
Seeing a different movie
Cause neither of us were ever on Time
Playing basketball @ the Y when we weren't kissing
Looking 4 an empty room @ the Y 2 kiss
Laying by the lake watching the ducks go by
A Million memories & more, yet
If Lose This Picture May Never C U Again...

LOVE POEM #1

PUREST LOVE
MELTING GLACIER ICE
ERUPTING SPITTING FIRE
CAN'T BURN ME AS MUCH AS THOSE EYES.
SOMETHING I'LL REMEMBER
TRUTH. ETERNITY.

LOVE POEM #2 (SWAHILI)

MASKINI AU MALKIA
YOTE SAWA
U KAMA MUNGU KWA MACHO YANGU
MASKIO YANGU AMEPENDEZWA NA JINA LAKO

Love Poem # 3 (Croatian)

IAKO JE MLADA DUSA
JA IPAK ZNAM
DA SI TI POSTAO MOJ ZRAK
ALI I DALJE NE ZNAM KAKO DISATI U TVOJOJ PRISUTNOSTI

Love Poem #4 (Latin)

Quod Sulum Vicis Nos Opportunus.
Memor Mihi Inde.
Quod Sulum Vicis EGO Licentia.
Memor EGO Sum Hic.

Love Poem #5 (Arabic)

في هذه الحياة. مع هاتان العينان
يبقى أن أرى البحر
لكن بوظوح , شواطئها
أضعك في اطار شيء أقرب لحقيقية لحلم

Love Poem # 6 (Chinese)

暮霭，烟花，晨曦
那些地方我从未去
但是我在家里
因为你在这里

or

日落，焰火，日出，
未曾到過的地方
而我是在家中，
正因爲這裡有你。

Riluo, yanhuo, richu,
Wei ceng dao guo de difang.
Er wo shi zai jiazhong,
Zheng yinwei zheli you ni.

Love Poem # 7 (Hindi)

Lakhon Ki Duniya Hai
Lekin Bhid Main Tujhe Pahechan Lunga.
Chahe Lakhon Aawaz Gunjte Rahe
Teri Chupki Si Aawaz Sun Lunga

Love Poem #8 (Portuguese)

Rodei-me, Esfriame, Aqueça-me
Com o seu sol de penetrção. E a sua brisa resfriando.
Faça-me forte simultaneamente no seu coração…
E fraco joelhos nós

Love Poem #9 (Russian)

И опять в первый раз,
Замороженные крохотные капли,
Испоряются от твоего прикосновения.
Эмоции вскипают и судьба захватывает тебя.

Love Poem #10 (Korean)

외모의 변화는 한결같이 유지된다.
그러나 영혼은 똑같이 그대로다.
해안과 일몰의 모습은 변화한다.
그러나 당신의 눈빛은 변함이 없다.

```
WE MO NUN GGUN IM UB SI BYUN HA JI MAN
YOUNG HON EUN GEU DAE RO YA.
HAE BYUN GWA IL MOL E BYUN HAE DO
NI NUN I BO NEUN GUN BYUN DAM UB SEO
```

Love Poem #11 (Japanese)

吸い込んで、紅潮する。
息を吐いて、涼しい。
当時、御目に掛かった事だけでなく、
二度三度私を見つける事も光栄。

suikonde, kouchousuru.
iki o haite, suzushii
touji, ome ni kakatta koto dake denaku,
nidosando watashi o mitsukeru koto mo kouei.

—Translation help in its entirety, done by Emily Souza

Love Poem #12 (German)

Du bist nicht nur mein schicksal.
Sie Sind Mein Schicksal, Und Mehr
Liebe bildet Herzen bluten Karma durch meine Adern.
Zu Ihre Ankunft sicherstellen, wie ich warte.

Love Poem # 13 (Italia)

Felicità. Fedeltà. Rispetto.
Ancora il mio compito è ancora da fare.
L'eternità è non venire.
Ogni esistenza è il vostro cuore ancora essere vinta.

Love Poem #14 (Espanol)

Lindo se Convierte en Hermoso
Elamor Como el Fuego Quema el Agua
Derrite Corazones Como el Chocolate
Vamos a ir a Sol Amarillo en la Playa. Esta Vez Mas Caliente . . .

Love Poem #15 (Français)

Somnolent je deviens.
Pour vous voir seulement là aussi.
Quand je me réveille trouvez-moi.
Bien que si je ne fais pas, par la réincarnation je vous trouve

LOVE POEM #16

GANG PÅ GANG
VEJO O AMOR A PRIMEIRA VISTA . . .
AKO NG MGA MINAMAHAL MO BAGO.
E O AMAREI NOVAMENTE.
KONPLÈ, BÈL, RÈV
ADIÓS MI AMOR.
JE VOUS VERRAI DANS LA MA VIE PROCHAINE.
JE VOUS AIMERAI DANS CELUI-LÀ.
AND I'LL LOVE YOU IN THIS LIFE TOO.

& THAT'S Y I HURT . . .

WHEN U FIRST CAME IN2 MY LIFE
U MAY NOT HAVE BEEN EXACTLY WHAT I EXPECTED,
THOUGHT U WOULD B,
OR EVEN WANTED U 2 B . . .

BUT YET, KNEW FROM THE MOMENT I SAW U
I HAD A LOVE IN MY HEART 4 U
THAT NO-1 ELSE, COULD EVER HAVE

AS WE GREW OLDER 2-GETHER
I HATED THAT I ALWAYS HAD 2 B THE 1
2 SHOW I ACTUALLY CARED ABOUT U,
& DO WHAT WAS BEST 4 U

I NEVER SHOWED U $$$ 2 PROVE I LOVED U.
NEVER LET U HAVE ALL THE FUN U WANTED 2, OR
GAVE IN2 YOUR CUTE SMILE CAUSE I
WANTED SOME-1 TO LOVE ME OR
EVEN JUST LIKE ME.

I NEVER DID THAT, AND NEVER WANTED 2,
4 THE REASONS OTHERS DID.
I LOVED U 2 MUCH 2 GIVE U EVERYTHING U WANTED,
BUT DID EVERYTHING, 2 GIVE U EVERYTHING U NEEDED

WHEN I GAVE U SOMETHING, IT WAS BECAUSE I LOVED U
NOT CAUSE I WANTED U 2 LOVE ME
I SPENT TIME WITH U, BECAUSE I LIKED U
NOT CAUSE I WANTED U 2 LIKE ME

AS WE GOT OLDER, WE ALL CHANGED.
THOUGH OTHERS INTENTIONS DID NOT.
STILL EXPECTING U 2 FULFILL THEIR NEEDS WITHOUT
FULFILLING YOURS.

I NEVER EXPECTED ANYTHING FROM U, EXCEPT 4,
WHAT WAS BEST 4 U . . .

I'M NO LONGER ON THE INSIDE,
BUT RATHER LOOKING IN
WHICH I'M FINE WITH, EXCEPT THAT
IT'S NOT WHAT'S BEST 4 U

U MADE A MISTAKE,
WHEN U TOOK MY KINDNESS 4 GRANTED, BUT
HEY WE ALL MAKE MISTAKES
BUT WHEN U ACT AS IF U COULD CARE LESS,
I FEEL U DON'T FEEL AT ALL BAD
& THAT'S Y I HURT . . .

WHEN I SEE THE PEOPLE AROUND U
GIVING U, WHAT U SAY U WANT
SO THEY CAN GET WHAT THEY WANT OR
LETTING U DO WHAT U WANT
SO THEY CAN DO WHAT THEY WANT
IT BURNS A HOLE IN MY HEART
& THAT'S Y I HURT . . .

WHEN I C U,
I C SOME-1 WHO,
NO LONGER BELIEVES THEY R BEAUTIFUL,
ON THE INSIDE & THE OUTSIDE
& THAT'S Y I HURT . . .

WHEN I HEAR YOUR VOICE
YOUR VOICE STILL MAKES ME SMILE
YET, I HEAR SOME-1 WHO'S GIVEN UP
& THAT'S Y I HURT . . .

WE ALWAYS KNEW U COULD DO HUGE THINGS YET
WHEN U SPEAK, U MAKE ME BELIEVE,
THAT U NO LONGER BELIEVE
& THAT'S Y I HURT . . .

I LOVE U SO MUCH THAT I ALWAYS
TELL U WHEN I DON'T AGREE WITH WHAT U DO

HOW U ACT
WHAT U SAY, THINK, OR BELIEVE
YET U THINK, I HAVE AN ULTERIOR MOTIVE 4 IT
& THAT'S Y I HURT . . .

I'VE ALWAYS BEEN THE 1 THAT WOULD UNDERSTAND.
THE 1, ALWAYS ON YOUR SIDE, ESPECIALLY
WHEN OTHERS WERE AGAINST U.
YET NOW U THINK I'M THE ONE AGAINST U
& THAT'S Y I HURT . . .

YET I'M THE SAME PERSON THAT
LOVED WHEN U FELL ASLEEP IN MY ARMS
THE SAME PERSON THAT WOULD DIVE
IN2 THE BELLY OF THE BEAST JUST 2 C U
THE SAME PERSON THAT CRIED EVERY NIGHT
I COULDN'T COME C U 4 THE FIRST TIME IN MY LIFE
YET I FEEL U BELIEVE THAT I NO LONGER CARE
& THAT'S Y I HURT . . .

U ALWAYS LOVED THAT I ALWAYS NEW WHAT 2 DO &
NOW I C U MAKING MISTAKES I KNOW U'LL END UP
REGRETTING
AND 4 THE FIRST TIME I DON'T KNOW WHAT 2 DO 2 HELP U
& THAT'S Y I HURT . . .

I ONCE TOLD U IF I EVER HAD KIDS
I'D WANT THEM 2 B JUST LIKE U
YET I DON'T KNOW WHAT 2 START WITH WHEN WE TALK
AGAIN
EVEN WORSE I DON'T KNOW IF U WANT 2 SPEAK AGAIN
& THAT'S Y I HURT . . .

We were supposed 2 grow old 2gether but I didn't have a chance

It wasn't meant 4 me
Not This time around
I'll C U In my next life
I'm fighting Till The end
But The end Is closing In
I'll B looking 4 U
Next time around
Eventually
It'll B Meant 2 B
Search & find
Don't wait 4 me
But I'll B Waiting 4 U
Eye's R getting heavy
It's time 2 go~^~^^~^~^~~
Next time . . . We'll grow old . . . _____

I wanna write U a song

I wanna write U a song
I'd start with a line that catches your attention
Like a cop rolling up next 2 U
Then start it off with a line so silky
The Saxophone in the background gets jealous
It's coupled with a slow bass line
That gets faster as the temperature rises
I wanna write U a song
With a verse so smooth & soft
It can make your heart drop so fast, it gets lost
I'd make it so deep 2 your soul
I could call it Grand Canyon in D
I wanna write U a song
That has a refrain so blissful
It makes onions envious
With a voice so beautiful
Billie Holiday or Aaliyah
Could have came back 2 earth 2 sing it
I wanna write U a song
With a climax so high
The Himalayas have an orgasm
I wanna write U a song
With a beat, lyric & poem so perfect
U have 2 turn the needle back,
Press rewind or skip back 2 hear it again

Y Don't U Want Me

Y Don't U Want Me
    Cause I Know That U Do
I Can C It In Your Eyes
    When U Playfully
        Pillow Fight With Me
I Can Hear It In Your Voice
    When We Talk All Night
I Can Feel Your Heart Beat Faster
    When U Hug Me
I Tell U I Have Feelings 4 U
    And I Can Here The
        Happiness In Your Voice
But U Hesitate 2 Say It Back
Y Don't U Want Me
    Cause I Know That U Do
Maybe U Don't Believe Me
    But My Words R Sincere
Maybe U Feel Yours R Stronger
    & U Feel The Need 2 Act Like
        U Don't Want Me
Cause I Know That U Do

There's Nothing 4 Me Here, Except U—4
Ashlee my baby sister

The Streets Of NYC R Calling Me
As R The Waves Of San Juan
The Pools In Orlando Call Me Back
As Does The Balloons In Albuquerque
The Oasis Of Las Vegas Screams 4 Me
As Does The Chicago Cuisine
San Diego Tells Me Now
As Does Places I've Never Seen
There's 2 Many Things
I Feel I Must See
But Without U
I Wouldn't Feel Complete

My Dreams

I'm here cause your eyes are mysterious
I'm here cause your lips look succulent
I'm here cause your skin appears delicate
I'm here cause of your hair looks spun of silk
I'm here cause of your lioness walk towards me
I'm here cause our heat melts gold
I'm here cause I can only speculate these presumptions
I'm here cause it's all in theory
I'm here cause I dream of you constantly
I'm here to find out the truth
I'm here cause my dreams need detail

UGLY BEAUTY 1

U said it 1nce
It didn't make any sense
U said it 1nce
& haven't said it since
I know U do
But I don't know to what Degree
Say it again
Or something in the vicinity
Say something soon
Or show something to make me believe
Say it soon
Before I have to leave

U say I said it Before
But I don't think I did
U say I said it Before
If I hadn't, I wish I Did
I know I Always have
At least to some degree
Cause every thought of you
Is In that vicinity
I wanted to say it eye to eye
Give you a reason to believe
I want to say it eye to eye
So tell me when to leave

<u>I'm glad I told you</u>
<u>That hot August Night</u>
<u>I'm glad I told you</u>
<u>But The Way Wasn't Right</u>
<u>U didn't want To Hear it Now, I know</u>
<u>Cause well, We're Geographically not close</u>
<u>But I Had To Tell U Now</u>
<u>Cause Now, U needed to hear it most.</u>

HIT BY A BUS

The Puzzle is Still Unfinished
But Now it's Getting Close To Done
Almost Figured it Out
Five, Ten, Fifteen plus years later
But Never Had All The Pieces Until Now
Call Me Crazy But You're the Last Piece To The Puzzle
Confusing as it was
Some Clues I never Understood Til Now
Others I didn't know were clues til Now
I never Knew why I liked Unagi Before I ever tried it
I couldn't understand why I would cringe anytime a bus
       went by me. Close Enough that I could feel the breeze
            it would make.
Never noticed the connection with the sudden back pain it
       would give me after it went by.
Come To think of it, I never knew why I knew multiple
       facts about bamboo, dragons and etc. That I knew I
            had never read in a book before, cause well That would
                have required me to have read books, +
I know I didn't hear it in schools cause that requires
       them to teach about other cultures + other history than
            "their" own. It would also require the history
                + culture they teach to also be true + factual.
Many clues more + yet still confused more
Wondering Why When I took a Japanese Class it came
       so easy until I learned one phrase, + After that
            one phrase no matter how hard I tried that
                was the only words that stuck in my head
+ now you, my final clue, cause I remember those
eyes. Piercing through me again.
call me crazy but now I put the puzzle together
Your Eyes, The Phrase, + A Bus Racing By . . .
The Bus Hit Me After seeing Those Eyes of Yours

But Not Before I said The Only phrase I
Can now remember in That Language
"Denwa Bango Nanban Deska"
So Here we meet again, in Another Life
But This time No BUS . . . Please . . .
So Let's Try This one More Time. As I step Away From
The Street . . .
"What's Your phone #"

Fake Poem #1

👁'm Over U
Yeah I Know I've said this B4
       & I took U Back B4 a couple times
But this time it's over 4 real
+ not because this time it was your decision
+ not just because you did something wrong
      like the previous times + I had to break it off
           just for the principle of the situation
                 + had to keep my integrity among my friends + so
I'm over you cause I really am
Now I know what you're thinking
      "If I'm over you, Why am I writing about U"
Well that's a good Question, cause I'm not
      even thinking about U NEMore
but I wrote this cause I'm an artist, a poet
even though I only had really written about U B4
      and I don't do open mics or keep a book or journal
         of my stuff.
This is just a poem, I decided to write, to let
      everyone know how bad of a person U R
And the only reason I'm not using your name in
      this poem is because, well, I'm not using your name in
         it for your sake. Not because I don't want everyone out
           there 2 know you're single now
Cause I ain't even thinking about that
I mean, I ain't even thinking about you
+ the only reason this poem is so long is
      cause I wanna make sure U know, I'm over U
I mean I've 4gotten all about U
I don't even remember what "our song" was
Yeah! that's right
I just 4got it
Which U probably don't even remember what it was
It was "Luv U 4 Life" by Jodeci in case you forgot
You know song #2 on the mixtape I made U
      on our 2 and a half week anniversary, that by the way . . . you forgot

And About our 6 month anniversary that would have been
      in two weeks, 11 days to be exact. I don't even
          care . . .
              Yeah
Because I'm over you
I don't even think about U at night.
      Except for When I see the picture of us by the bed
          but that's because of the picture not cause I'm
              thinking of you.
And I Have the picture up because I look good in the picture
      And I Just don't have the time to crop out your picture,
And reprint it . . .
Oh + just so you know I erased your number out of
      my phone
Yeah I know your names still in it but your cell
number is erased. And I only kept your work number
in there cause you work at Macy's + I'm waiting for that
jacket to go on sale, + your not the only one who answers
that phone, especially on Fridays + Saturdays when you're not
working or before 10 or after 5:30 on the other days
+ I didn't erase your email out of it cause I forgot to +
I haven't gotten around to it again. So Yeah to Sum it up
I'm over U. period. End of discussion. Nothing more 2
B said. So Bye! Peace. I'm Gone.
And Another Thing . . .
    Just so U know
        It didn't even bother me that U wasn't
            replying to all of my text messages. You
                Know, before I erased your cell from
                    my phone . . . cause
    I really didn't wanna hear from you. I just
        wanted to show my friends how childish you
            were acting and why it was so easy for me to be over
                you. Cause it is . . . See watch one last
Time, to prove to everyone you never cared, because
U won't even answer . . . 612-483-*   *   *
I'm really good with numbers so what? "Hey what's up? Just
calling to see how you're doing. Call me when you get this."
    See You won't call . . .

Off Limits, No More

The Limit Was There
The Limit Was Clear
The Limit Made It Unthinkable
Unthinkable, But Not In a Bad Way
Unthinkable Cause The Idea Never Formulated
It Was Never An Option
Never Needed To Wonder
Cause It Never Was A Choice
Never On The Table
Never A Possible Selection
Never A Focus For My Possible Affection
Not Really Off The Table
Cause You Never Were On It
Therefore Never An Object For Something More
Than You Were To Me Then
But Today The Sun Didn't Set Exactly As Expected
The Tide Didn't Turn The Same
And The Stars Were Aligned Differently
Something Was Different
The Light Came Upon You Differently
Therefore Making Me See You In A Different Light . . .
You Always Meant Something To Me
But Now The Constraints Are Broken
The Reason(s) No More
No Longer Off Limits
So We Could Possibly Be More

All Stunned

I Ain't Gonna Make It
I Won't B There
So I Won't C U 2Nite—
    Like We Planned
I Don't Wanna Cancel Again—
    But I Kinda ½ 2
I Won't C U 2Nite—
    2Morrow
        Or Probably NE-Time Soon
I Know You're Probably Upset That I Have 2 Cancel Again
Probably Questioning My Reasons
Wondering If I'm Finding Reasons—
    Not 2 C U
My Reasons R Real—
    Valid—
        & I Know U Do Understand
I Wanna C U 2Nite
More Than U Probably Know
& That's Y
    I Won't C U 2Nite
That's Y I Have 2
    Text U Instead Of Calling
Because If I Call U—
    & Hear Your Voice
I'll Probably Show
& God Knows I Ain't Ready 4 That
See When I Hear Your Voice
    It Does Something 2 Me I Can't Explain
+ When I C Those Eyes
    It Makes Me Defenseless Inside
& If U Look In2 Mine—
    & Say, Just 1 Word
I'll Rush In2—
    Everything I'm Desperately Trying 2 Wait 4
Cause With U—
    I Know I Can't Say No—

        Cause Well, I Don't Want 2
I Don't Want 2 Wait 2 C U—
    Or NE-Thing That Will Come Along With That
But I Won't C U 2Nite
    Cause U Make My Mind & Body—
        Do & Feel Things Nothing Can Explain
You Make Me Touch Emotions—
    & See Air—
        Leaving Me Speechless & All Stunned
Confused, I
    See Air,
I Am,
    All Stunned
Senses Only C, Feel
    See Air, All Stunned

Sexiest one ever . . .

I have 100 reasons not to talk to you . . . 100 friends telling me I'm crazy, and that I need to get as far away as possible from you . . . But let's be honest, you're the hottest stalker I ever had . . . Now I've had other hot stalkers before, but you take it to a whole new level . . . Plus you're way more dedicated than the others. And I can admire someone who puts their all into something. That's respectable . . . The dedication (not the stalking, that is) now sure I could easily get a restraining order, but the thought of you restraining me, ain't that bad . . . I mean I'm sure part of me would be a little terrified but I'd also be comforted by your hotness . . . Now this is where my friends tell me how crazy I sound . . . But let's face it, some of them didn't even make to my last birthday party but when I looked across the room, there you were gazing back at me. And you weren't even invited, yet there you were, talking to all my friends trying to get to know everything about me that you could. You make me feel like a leader cause where ever I go . . . you follow. You make me feel beautiful cause you hang up pictures of me like I used to hang pictures of Halle Berry. You make me feel safe, cause I always know someone is watching my back. Now friends may come and go but a good stalker will always stay . . . If I was hit by a car and fell into a coma, I have no doubt you would be there nursing me back to health, if I went prison I know you'd be there waiting for me, cause well you show up everywhere else, why not for conjugals too? Now I must remind you that I'm not condoning your infatuation with me. I've just decided that because of how unbelievably hot and gorgeous you are I was going to accept it and roll with it cause well your just that fine!!! You're beautiful and I love everything about you. From your athletic ability to keep up with me on my morning runs, to you gorgeous hair blowing in the wind as you track me down on a windy day, I love your starlight eyes that sparkle outside my windows at night, and your very sexy legs that have become even more luscious as your dedication to follow me has grown. I love your sleek, sexy, toned binocular holding arms, and your constant picturing taking makes me feel like a movie star. Your intelligent problem solving techniques show how smart you are, as you found my web page and cell number even though I didn't give them to you, and I'm a sucker for an intellectual girl. And when I'm having a bad day, the multiple text messages remind me that there is someone out their thinking about me, and on nights that

I can't sleep, your very, very, very long voicemails always do the trick as the explicit ones wake me up in the morning when I just don't wanna go to work. You are the sexiest stalker I ever had, and I know you're very understanding as my schedule changes often, yet you're always there for me. So with that said, I only request 3 things from you . . . When you playfully sneak into my house and spray my pillows with your perfume to ensure I think of you as I sleep, please only mist it once, or ill cough all night long . . . Two . . . Please don't start stalking me until 8:05, as much as I like the attention from a beautiful lady, I'm tired of hearing my boss ask me why you can get to my job on time but I can't . . . And thirdly . . . And probably most importantly . . . When I'm taking a shower please don't stare from outside the bathroom window and watch. Just come in and join me . . . I'll leave the doors unlocked, cause, after all, you are the hottest stalker I ever had . . . Well I gotta run, but you already knew that didn't you . . .

Ugly Beauty 2

You can say whatever you want
Intentions are both good
You can say whatever you want
Where are feelings stand and stood
Tell me how you feel
And I'll tell you what you've wanted to hear
But you say don't say that
Cause it'll be a long time before you're here

The Poem Version 2 (The Long Lost Version)

Purest Love
Melting Glacier Ice
Erupting Spitting Fire
Can't Burn Me As Much As Those Eyes.
Something I'll Remember
Truth. Eternity.

    Peasant Or Queen
    It's All the Same
    Goddess In My Eyes
    My Ears Developed A Love For Your Name.

Young Soul Still
Yet Each Time I Knew
You Become My Air
But I Still Don't Know How To Breathe Around You.

    And Each Time We Meet
    Remember Me From There
    And Each Time I Leave
    Remember I Am Here

In This Life. With These Eyes.
I Have Yet To See The Sea.
But Vividly, Beaches . . .
Frame You In Something To Real To Dream.

    Sunset. Fireworks. Sunrise.
    Places I've Never Been.
    Yet I'm Home
    Cause Here You Are Again.

Land Of Millions.
I Can Find You In The Crowd.
A Million Voices Talking.

But I Hear Your Whisper Loud.

> Surround Me. Cool Me. Warm Me.
> With Your Penetrating Sun And Your Cooling Breeze.
> Make Me Simultaneously Strong In The Heart
> And Weak In The Knees.

Here Again For The First Time.
Miniscule Water Frozen.
Evaporates With Your Touch.
Emotions Rush In And Fate Pulls In.

> Change In Appearance Stays Constant.
> But Soul Stays The Same
> View Of The Shore And Sunset Transform.
> But The Look From Your Eyes Remain.

It Burns Each Breath I Breathe.
Yet Cools Each Exhale That Leaves
The Honor Wasn't Just In Meeting You Back Then.
The Honor Is, You Finding Me Again And Again.

> For You Are Not Just My Destiny.
> You Are My Fate.
> Love Makes Hearts Bleed Karma Through My Veins.
> To Ensure Your Arrival As I Wait.

Happiness. Loyalty. Respect.
Still My Job Is Yet To Be Done.
Eternity Has Not Come.
Each Existence Has Your Heart Yet To Be Won.

> Pretty Becomes Beautiful.
> Love Like Fire Burns Water.
> Melts Hearts Like Chocolate.

Let's Go To Yellow Sun On the Beach. This Time Much Hotter . . .

Sleepy I Become.
Only To See You There Too.
When I Wake Find Me.
Though If I Don't, Through Reincarnation I Will Find You.

. . .
Time After Time
I See Love At First Sight
I Have Loved You Many Times Before.
And I'll Love You Again.
Complete, Beautiful, Dream
Goodbye My Love.
I'll See You In My Next Life.
I'll Love You In That One.
And I'll Love You In This Life Too.

Not even a start . . .

What do, in Haikus?
Cause seventeen syllables,
Ain't enough for you . . .

No Introduction Needed

Names irrelevant

Details, facts reappear cause,

Our souls met before

'MIXED' EMOTIONS CAN BE 100% REAL

Like the akki, I grow from ki
4 you're the ishkote that nindanakis . . . inside
The nodin that keeps me gikÂdjwin

My ishpiming I need to breathe
4 U touch me like gikÂdjiwin nibi on nindon
U R the missing bokwaii I desperately manêsiwin

In the form of an migisi
You're a Anjeni genawenimak watching over me with your otchitchhÂgoma

In my mind nind ojisidekawe following Ki
Nin Kotagiigon 2 know your with them nin nissitawendan
But knowing there might B ganas inside gives wanakiwidéewin
Still nind atÂwe mi corazon for yours
But you're still with him nin dassôs

If I could not make U happy
I'd bite my love, pride and would not try
But I've been there B-4 and have seen things mess In hopes that soon U, I'll B with
but I've progressed moved my pawns and found the Queen
chess (mate in 36) and in the dream I could not C the color
of ones dress but what I know I saw was happiness

I want a piece of your heart and soul
but I'm not selfish
4 I'll give you mine

I felt your soul touch mine
I felt my soul touch yours

\+ (still) Amazingly close (and lived through time)
    4 that there's no bond that ties
        aside from a/the love that underlies

A stranger told me the answer is in front of me. "Your soul is tired, let it rest.
        do not try to bring 2 light your place for you already know
        where it is. Any advice now is irrelevant but needed as the
        answer will be reconstructed to fit the question at hand . . ."
He then replied to my telepathic question "Your heart is your home"
no wonder I'm homesick
cause es tu mi corazon

In The Closet

I can see in your eyes   we want to give it
You're my fantasy (and)   👁 want 2 live it
U can have me   if you're willing
U got a man (but)   👁 C no fillin'

I got this desire,   👁 can not hide it
I tried it,   👁 can't deny it my heart C's it
I want U   my body cry's it
I want U   J'ai besoin de vous
         (Le) Tu Necessito

kept these feelings, In the closet
Caught up, U lied we think he bought it
I fill him with jealousy   (*He doesn't even know*)
(He can feel it though cause)   He can't even look at me

         Je comprends finalement
         La vérité de desire
         femme à l'homme

I want U   (¿Porque no me llamas?)
U want me 2 (*no drama*)
U got this body (I'm startin 2 lust it)
I got this lust (I'm startin 2 love it)
U got this passion /inside/ (well let me rub it)
U got this feeling /2/ (U need 2 trust it)
(Is it) lust or love (👁 want to kick it)
👁 C your neck (👁 want 2 kiss it)
👁 C your thighs (👁 want to lick it)
Yo tengo amor (please don't miss it)
👁 C your lips (👁 want to taste it)
J'ai cette passion (don't let me waste it)

3 Strikes

Like a needle to my veins,
it executes me quickly,
yet not quick enough.
I look through the glass
& the thought of seeing you kills me.
Scales over my eyes couldn't
stop me from seeing something
so sharp, it cuts my heart,
making it all race through my veins.
No antidote for something
seemingly written in stone.
For even if there was,
I have no doubt, the venom
would kill me before I
could even push the air out
the pinpoint steel thorn.
Before the phone could ring
to tell them to keep the venom out
of my bloodstream that runs through
every part of my body that
remembers you.
For if, for some reason, the venom
runs through my system and only kills
the body I borrow this time around;
the legs that help me stand,
the neck that keeps my eyes looking up,
and the heart that pumps blood
to every part of my brain
that bears a memory of you.
If all I have, is what's left after that,
the time will kill my soul.
Knowing you're so close,
yet not being able to
stay with you each time I see you
will steal each breath I try to breathe.
These bars between us,

seemingly, will kill my heart,
take my soul,
and steal my air.
I continue to do time,
as I bleed/plead guilty
to knowing our souls touched,
yet it feels like the crime is against me.
So I accept the sentence, for
I can't be free, even if I'm not the one
who is restrained.
Take your time,
Confined you may be,
but as you are, as you stay.
I am held in a cell also.
Just cause no bars or cuffs
incarcerate me,
I learn that,
if you are locked away
I do not have be imprisoned,
to be locked up too.

I'll wait forever...oo

You say you love yourself some me
Yet you can't you leave with me tonight . . .
Each promise he makes you
Only reminds you, how I
Can promise you more.
And when I do nothing to stop you,
As I always respect your unspoken decision,
It only makes you look back, each time you leave.

Stare at me over his shoulder when you dance,
Exhale deeply when you wanna come over to me
But you know you shouldn't.
Smile deeper inside, than the already wide grin
You give me, each time you say hi to me up close.

Dream deep in my eyes,
And get lost in my thoughts momentarily,
Cause you know I am briefly doing the same in
The small window of opportunity we have
As we pass by each other's gaze.

Make each hug you give more intimate than the last,
And each time you get better at concealing
How intense each embrace is becoming.
Go ahead and melt more each time we clasp together,
For I know, I have to catch you each time you fall,
For you say, my arms, makes your soul exhausted,
Makes your legs crumble.
Fall, cause you know I'll catch you,
& pick you up each time.

Consider the open-ended option briefly.
Say no for now, and sleep on it.
Keep all the love you bleed buried,
The unconscious and conscious secrets
In your heart . . . to ourselves . . .

Even if you, forever wanna hide it.
Cause I believe, that one-day.
Whenever you call.
On that day.
This time.
You will have something different to say.

Nothing before has been clearer, cause time
Has not gradually diminished "us"
When, instead this passion,
Has faded the time.
The stars prove it's not the end,
Because the line between us,
Makes each time we look into each other's eyes,
Feel like the first all over again.

I'll wait forever,
      cause you know,
that you won't make me wait that long . . .

Chapter 9

Thoughts To Ponder

These are my thoughts, <u>what are yours?</u> **Have mine changed over time?** *Have yours? Which are theories/thoughts*, **<u>which are facts?</u>**

I BELIEVE

I don't believe in love at first sight or that
you can always count on somebody I
don't believe truly broken hearts ever heal
completely or you can go through your whole
life thinking everybody you need will some-
day let you down but I do believe the
word <u>Love</u> is overused and sometimes
has no meaning
      I don't believe children are dumb, or that
I know everything I don't believe rap music
causes violence or that chocolate is a
substitute for sex but I do believe that life
should be fun
      I don't believe people ever want to die,
or that Minneapolis is a rough place I don't
believe that the majority of us know what
love is or that you can break a habit I don't
believe that sleeping less than 10 hours makes
you tired or that making love and having sex
are the same I do believe you get what
you deserve
      I don't believe that I'm a waste of
talent or that I'm irresponsible I don't
believe school is useful or that because I
don't do my homework I won't make it but
I do believe that I will succeed
      I don't believe I will ever see certain people
again or that I'm always right I don't be-
lieve what others think of me I don't believe
people should hide their ideas or that it's not
O.K. to cry But I do believe that in time
someday I will love again.

What you really mean . . .

<u>I'm confused—</u>
      Don't pin me down
<u>I'll try—</u>
      I don't expect to succeed
<u>I can't decide—</u>
      I will not decide
<u>But . . .—</u>
      I deny what I just said
<u>I'm frustrated—</u>
      I'm unwilling to tolerate this
<u>I've got a conflict—</u>
      I don't want to choose, I want
      to have them both
<u>I don't know—</u>
      I won't tell you
<u>I'm only human—</u>
      I don't have much respect for
      myself
<u>I don't care—</u>
      I care very much but I don't want
      others to know
<u>I used to be—</u>
      I still am
<u>I don't know—</u>
      So you tell me
<u>You aren't being cooperative—</u>
      You're not doing what I want you to
<u>I'm ambivalent—</u>
      I want both, I don't want to choose
<u>I expect a lot from others—</u>
      I expect perfection from myself
<u>It's a habit—</u>
      I am a victim
<u>Except—</u>
      I deny what I just said

<u>I'm not ready for</u>—
>   I'm not willing to

<u>I don't know</u>—
>   I don't want to commit myself

<u>I can't decide</u>—
>   I will not decide

<u>I should . . .</u>=
>   I know what I should do, but I
>   am reluctant to do it

<u>Nothing's wrong</u>—
>   Leave me alone

<u>I feel threatened</u>—
>   I'm afraid I'm losing control

<u>Your wrong</u>—
>   I don't believe you

<u>However . . .</u>=
>   I deny what I just said

<u>It's not logical</u>—
>   It doesn't suit me

<u>It's a habit . . .</u>=
>   and I don't plan to change it

<u>I have no ambition</u>—
>   I don't want to do it

<u>Nothings wrong</u>—
>   Something wrong, but I don't want
>   you to know what it is

<u>You're my last hope</u>—
>   and I expect to defeat you too.

The secret to Life, that you forgot

Remember when you were a kid full of joy
      and innocence
You didn't even know what the words meant
You built castles with your blocks and would
      Knock your brothers towers down and laugh
You played house with your dolls
"Shh, Be Quiet! My baby's sleep" you said, It was
      so much fun
But each year you were greeted with more re-
      sponsibilities and you slowly forgot how to have
      fun
Now you talk about how much fun childhood was
And now it's time to be a child again,
I mean have fun
      Color outside the lines go ahead It's fun
Hang it on the fridge even though the faces
      are purple and their arms are green
When a mom sees it she'll say it's beautiful
      and then you'll smile
Believe in Santa, Remember how fun it was
Playing with G.I. Joes and Ninja Turtles, going
      to birthday parties and playing with the
      toy you got them
It was fun
Get up early tomorrow for school cause you
      can't wait to play kickball at recess
      or to have snack time
See how much candy you can eat on Halloween
I tell you to ride your bike everywhere you go
      tomorrow
To tell a dumb joke "What did the farmer say
      when he lost his tractor"—Where's my
      tractor!
But you hesitate to do it,
You're afraid, but I understand
But remember that childhood was fun cause

      you were creative and did new things
Remember the times you remember are the
      times you tried something new
But now you're repetitive
So I say try something new
Whether it's making grits, black-eyed peas and
      chicken for breakfast or go bowling or
           ice-skating if it's the first you'll remember it
You forgot that the best thing in life is
      having fun

Double Vision
The same words used in different orders create a different truth!

The Glass is Half Empty

I look 2 the future.
  With the exception of this moment,
  It's All 👁 Have Left

*T*hough my past is coming,
  👁 Still Have time Left . . .
  When It Comes It May Not Matter

4 if my past catches the present
  it may become my future
  making my future the present
  but in actuality it will B my Past

4 if it's all the same it
  cannot be different. If the Past
  touches the present it becomes
the past turning the future into the Present

*S*o if It's all the same, then
  There is no past or present, and
  Worse there is no future. If there
Is no future then your time is up . . .

U can not hide your past . . . That's
  When it comes 2 get U . . . ending your future But
  If U Dwell on The Past U Have No
Present. No Present or No Future . . .

*D*on't Run or Hide and U must NOT
  Dwell . . . Don't Look back, but do
  Not forget. Tricky it is 2 find a
Medium, but if I do I will have a
tomorrow, and it won't B My Past!
(If I Don't, I'll only be the past . . .)

The Glass Is Half Full

While The Present is Here
I Look 2 The Future Over There
Soon The Future Will Be Here
And The Present Will Be The Past Back There
When The Here Goes Back There
There Will Become Here
And 👁 Will C A New There
I Will Then Look At The New There
While Working 2 Improve My Here
If 👁 Improve My Here
👁'll Feel Better Looking Back There, →
When My There Becomes Here.
And Though My Here Will Look
Much Better Than It Did Back There
Every Time My There Becomes A Here
👁'll Simply Receive Another There
Which Will Again Look Much Brighter Than Here
But No Matter How Good Or Bad It Gets Here
There Will Always Hold Hope 4 A Better
Here . . .

Beautiful Disaster

Predicament number one
There you stand
Something tells me to run
But here I stand
How can I not look
At such a beautiful sight
Your details have me shook
And your smile burns bright
Never seen something
That can literally stop you in your tracks
To bad there's nothing
More to you than that
I heard you speak
And you don't have a thought you own
Why'd we have to meet?
I'd have been better to never known
Stupidity, lies, & ugliness
Things you have mastered
Wrapped in such loveliness
What a beautiful disaster

Beautiful Lies

Tell me it's beautiful
It never hurt you before
Tell me it's beautiful
Cause it's my souls tour
Tell me it's beautiful
Even if you don't understand
Tell me it's beautiful
Cause I did it by hand
Tell me it's beautiful
Though you're not sure what it is
Tell me it's beautiful
Cause you know someone will think it is
Tell me it's beautiful
Cause it's ugly to perfection
Tell me it's beautiful
Cause it wasn't really a question
Tell me it's beautiful
Even if it's a lie
Tell me it's beautiful
& Look me in the eye . . .

An Adopted Misconception

You Didn't Save The World
& You Didn't Save Me.
I Was Not Dying When You Came Into My Life
& I Was Not Starving.
I Ate Everyday Just Like You
I Had Clothes On My Back &
I Had A Roof Over My Head.
The Food May Have Been Bad,
The Clothes A Little Worn,
& The Roof May Have Changed Frequently,
But I Was Never Without.
Your Intentions May Be Good,
But You Have Not Saved The World
& You Definitely Did Not Save Me.
I Always Had A Home &
I've Had "Parents" Too
The Homes May Have Been Many,
I've Grown Up As An Army Brat,
My Parents Just Weren't In The Military.
So You Did Not Save Me Nor Did You Save The World
It Was Not A Sacrifice For You To Bring Me Into Your Life
People Come Into Mine All The Time
The Sacrifice Will Be To Keep Me In It,
When I Give You No Reasons To Do So.
Cause You Have Not Saved The World
& You Did Not Save Me
I've Been Through This Before
It's Old News Repeated Again
You Want To Make A Difference In My Life?
Stay In It Cause I Haven't Seen That Yet.
You Don't Owe It To Me To Be A Good Parent,
That Was Never Your Obligation
You Want To Help Save The World?
Or At Least Change The View In Mine?
Be A Great Person . . .
So I Have Reason To Believe,
That There Are Other Great People Out There,
To Be Able To Trust They'll Stay Also

A 9.5 LOVE IN '95

I don't know how to express these feelings for you
        but it seems like no one understands me the way that you do
You see it's my girl and a beautiful temptation
        but could you understand the choice that I'm facin'
Cause when I see you my heart fills with hope
        If I go with my desires will I lose both
I want you to feel these feelings I feel
        Not sincerely but with love cause these feelings are real
I feel for you both and she'd always be by my side
        I have a passion for you but it's with her that I'm spending the nights
And every time I see you the airs filled with
        Infatuation, Lust and potential Love
I close my eyes my mind wanders free
        Every night you're the one I see
Thinking of you is how I'm spending the nights
        Except when I lay awake to think of your beautiful eyes
Looking in Brown for Brown
        I can't stop thinking of laying you down
I lay in her bed   another dream
        A night full of passion but its with you and me
I want to tell you about my feelings for you
        I'd do anything in this world just to be with you
I've been keeping these feelings inside
        so baby show me a sign
                that now is the right time

MORE THOUGHTS ABOUT A 9.5 LOVE IN '95

I sit and contemplate and into my daydreams you came
I know I belong with you and I hope your feelings are the same
I smile when I'm with you but at the same time my soul's full of pain
Cause deep inside it's my heart that seems to call out your name

Six Degrees of "I know you from somewhere..."

Coincidences connect us to the theory of fate, as it truly is a small world. No one really knows how many degrees separated us before we crossed paths the first time. However, if we separate, split paths, or lose our current connection: that being in the first degree. I know that, in no more than five more degrees we will meet again. In that day, it may seem like a coincidence, but the real coincidences will be the degrees that led us to meet again in this small yet chaotic feeling world.

I'll sleep when I'm dead!

Force is X
So if Time is Acceleration
That would make me Mass
Force then would = the impact I make when I do something great
Therefore sleep will only slow me down
Cause does Time really exist to the Mass if the Mass it not awake?
And if Time stops, the Acceleration stops.
Therefore lessoning the force of impact the Mass can make
So I then have no reason to sleep
If I want a Forcefully great impact . . .

but now,

I go to sleep, 4 the possibility, you'll be with me

My Philosophy—4 Victoria

Is life short or long? You may have your own opinion on this, but I tend to believe the future is long the past is short. Looking back you can't believe how fast things went by, yet tomorrow can seem like forever away. The real answer still lies in the fact that we all have multiple talents to display, a plethora of abilities to take advantage of... When we choose not to use these abilities stress builds and life is long, as there is too much time to fill, for the time were given to accomplish what we can is not being used... However, when we use each talent we possess life is short, cause in each talent we find out that we are capable of even more than previously thought. In turn that broadens our once tunnel vision to see all the other doors on our path that we can not only open but even create, build, or theorize. Take your idea. Make it happen. The Journey may seem long, but the future is much longer...

Chapter 10

Stories/Spoken Word

Spoken word and stories, like songs, are poetry. Not all, but most. Some times when writing poems they just take a story form. Sometimes the poem goes on much longer than you anticipated! So what would you classify it as? All of the above? To me it's still poetry, but it definitely has a story to go with it.

Someone heard a challenge to a great author to write a complete story in 6 words. That person looked at me and asked "Can you do it?" My goal was to write a complete story in 12 words, then another in 11 all the way down to six. But my mind and brain don't always listen to each other. So instead, here are ten stories, that tell a complete "story." **Do not read these stories back to back**. Take your time, & read one slowly, then take more time to think about it. Come back later and read the next one. Think about it, take a shower, or sleep on it.

Stories In 10 words or less . . .

Story #1

My Twin, Didn't Survive, Our Abortion . . .

I My Downfall
A. (I Had A Dream)

a. The other night I had a dream.
It wasn't one of those, "It feels real" dreams.
It's was one of those, this is, real, dreams.
It was one of those, it's not happening now, dreams,
    It's one of those, it's not,—happening,—now—dreams . . .
You know the kind, that's not happening now, now meaning, it's going to happen
Well I don't know when, but, it's going to happen cause this,—
Is a simulation, evaluation, preparation type dream.
One of those, you burn me with cigarette, or cut me with a knife type dreams
    And I wake up with the burn, the scar, to prove it type dreams.
This is a warning, a chance to see what's coming, type dreams . . .
The type of dream where you see a place you've never been before . . .
    But you remember the place, the stairway, and every detail type dreams.
        Only to later walk down the stairway years later &
            Say this is the stairway dream . . . The, I've been here before
            dream . . .
                Well never before the dream, but now here I am,
                  & This time, it's not a dream,
                      Type dreams.
            Cause See . . .
In the "Dream," a man in a mirror,
    Mirror image,
        Yet not mirroring me in this dream,
Is telling me my downfall type dream.
Pointing to all the people I'm seeing now, in this dream saying . . .
Your downfall is not thinking you can outsmart him.
Your downfall is not thinking you can outsmart Tony, Jared or Jim
Your downfall won't be thinking you can outsmart Julie, Katrina or Her
Being able to outsmart the average joe, the struggling, or the lady in fur.
    Cause well, let's be honest, we both know you can.
It won't be the police, a government official, or a politician,
It won't be the city bum, the killer, the hitman, or the disturbed mathematician.
It won't be you in the second row, or the one in the royal blue
It won't be you, you, you, or you . . .
It won't be the girl, who's here, with someone, who's not, her boyfriend . . .

It won't be the guy, who swears, she's, not, his girlfriend . . .
It won't be one of your enemies, the stranger,
        or any, one, of your close, best or casual friends.
Your downfall won't be thinking you can outsmart any one of them, any one of you . . .
We both know you can,—Outsmart—every—one—of them . . .
YOUR DOWNFALL, WILL BE . . . Thinking, that you, can outsmart, all of them . . .
. . . —Thinking, that I can outsmart,—**ALL**,—of you . . . Will be . . . my downfall . . .
So this is a warning type dream.
It could be real type dream, if you think this is just a dream, type dream.
Now wake up and go back to sleep, and dream, an actual, dream, type dream.
Cause well, this . . . —is a "to be continued . . ." type dream . . .

Story #2

Cancers Gone. Pain-Free. So Don't Cry.

Story #3

In Prison. Innocent. Yet I Belong.

II <u>My Downfall . . . Part 2</u>
A. <u>(I Had A Vision)</u>

1. I had a vision.
Not a dream, cause a vision . . .
Is much stronger than a dream.
Like someone with Extreme Insomnia
I never really was a sleep, never was really awake.
Manic Depressant, with Paranoia, migraine, damn my head hurts
But I come back before it gets worse . . .
10 years of memory, cram in 30 seconds
Someone's gonna walk through those doors in a few,
I don't know how I know but it's has you all shook.
Cause it was a vision, a flashback from the future.
I changed my past from 5 years from now from the dream I had, about my future back then.
Now I got a vision . . . cause well, this one's, more rushed . . .
I have a vision of my downfall. This time it's changed. This time it's not in my hands.
Well it is, but indirectly. Well kinda directly, depends if you're a chess player or you just play chess.
Cause this time my downfall is not whether or not I can outsmart you, you or you.
It's well, not as clear, cause this vision is . . . smokey, hazey, blurry, unclear.
Oh it's a clear vision, but that's just what the vision is, a cloud of smoke from a hot fire blurring my 30-20.
Another obstacle cause it's clear my downfall will be from this, but "this" can change or morph into this or this depending on how I first handle and respond the initial symptoms of the onslaught of "this," my downfall that is.
It's not whether I can outsmart the one responsible for my downfall. I outsmarted you already, many times, respectfully that is . . . To live for what I believe in the right way. Not speaking religiously by any means, but I'm religious about not doing that. Gotta believe in something and I can't help "you" with that. My downfall will be, whether all of "you" can stop yourselves from getting outsmarted

just once, or whether you just decide to give up, and make me do what you need, by giving me an offer I that I just can't refuse, but an offer that's well,—not even a choice. My downfall, will be a coin-flip, it's whether or not your pride stands in the ˏ ay. If it doesn't, I'm probably screwed. If your pride is your vice . . . I'm safe,—as long as I keeping walking, staying two steps ahead, looking out for dead end signs, and well, I'll need some luck too . . . Small-Odds, but I like My chances . . .

To be continued . . . ?

STORY #4

MOM NEVER TOLD DAD, THAT HE WAS A FATHER

Story #5

Dad Died Overseas, Before He Met Me.

Story #6

Nobody Knows. I Visited, Fell, With The Towers.

Story #7

Born. Mom Held Me. Then Fell Asleep, Forever . . .

II My Downfall
B.   A Second Vision

2. Another vision. Completely separate yet together.
Call it mistaken identity, or false imprisonment. Call it many things. Call it what it is, but it won't get written that way.
Ruin my name, lie, or think inside the box.
I won't be inside the box. I'll design from anywhere you choose, if I choose not to design, cause well, you hold all the cards.
I research and write, research and store in my head. I keep things in my head, cause people can't change what's stored their. You know that. I had a vision you used my research, to win your war with my destiny, my downfall.
My downfall just might be you,—using my research against me. The same research I'm doing to help educate and stop our "downfall as people . . ." To win your war, the war you don't even know why, who you're fighting. Don't know what, where your stand is. I'm not mad. Well I'm mad at the situation, cause it's not personal, but given the opportunity your ass is through. So I ask politely, before I give you my final offer . . . Give me my life . . . or be prepared to lose yours. Not a threat, not a warning. Cause honestly I have no idea, if MY downfall, will actually affect me, and make me fall down. But it's eminent, that some will fall, if you bring on, my downfall.

Story #8

God Said, "Much Better ... This Time ... "

Story #9

You'll Birth Me Today, Then Bury Me Tomorrow.

Story #10

It's Ok, That You'll Never Know, I've Always Loved You.

Story #11

Marry Me, In This Life Too . . .

Story #12

Soul Cries. Tomorrow. When You Marry.

Chapter 11

COVERING MY BASES

Well this is the smallest section of poems. You've seen many sides and layers to me. This section is small details about me, and poems to people who I wanted to make sure I didn't forget. Anything else I feel you should know is in this last section.

"Going Broke"

Talk about being broke
I Love Money like everyone else
So why does it seem like,
I`m the only one,
Money has filed a restraining order against?
Now I never abused Money, but
I guess you could say I did use her a lil` bit.
I try and patch things up.
But Money just hires lawyers,
Cause Money knows I can`t afford them myself.
I lost everything in the break up.
I couldn`t even get custody of the Change
Me and money made.
Money says I have an unfit home for Change,
Cause that circle in my money house,
Isn`t really a gold coin.
I guess you could say I got greedy.
And now I`m paying for it,
even though I can`t afford it.
They all knew about each other
But one day they all decided it was no longer ok
My Money one day, just ran out on me,
Money went to get groceries and hasn`t been back since ...
My Checks straight up left ... you know bounced ...
Even my stocks told me they had new options ...
But give me credit, I still got Credit.
Although I don`t think it`s legal, cause it
Costs me each time just to see her ...
In fact the only action I get is that nice
Stimulus package that needs to come back around again.
Now don`t get me wrong, I`m working overtime to get some new Money.
But it seems as though every time I get Money in my hands,
It`s gone before I can even spend time with it.
Now I won`t give up, but I realize it`s true what they say about love ...
It`s better to have had Money and lost it, than to have never had Money
at all ...

I AM . . . (1994)

I am the deck of cards that U don't know
      what's going to happen next
I am the Ladybug that gives people hope
I am the Basketball Jersey that is lost
      hoping to be found
I am the ticking bomb waiting to explode
      showing everyone what I can do
I am the Hurricane that no one can stop when
      I'm at my best
I am the Bear that doesn't use its power +
      strength until I have 2
I am the pen that writes the expression'
      the feeling
I am the feign barely getting by, yet
I am the rounder at the top of his game
I am the origin that contains The Pride, The
      Heart, The Soul
I am the Speech, The Song, The Spoken Word, The
      Poetry That Inspires and gives a reason
I am the nomad looking for a home
I am the Magic, Mysterious and totally unknown

If 👁 Should Die . . . —4 Michelle

If I should die this year
I will have shown and reaffirmed it in many ways
If I should die this season
I will have verified it through a sentimental gift
If I should die this month
You will have seen it in my eyes
If I die next week
I will have proved it in a hug or a touch
If I die tomorrow
I will have personally told you myself
If I should die today
At least finished this poem for you
To bare to you how much I cared

U R ME   4 Goofy, TNKRBELL, Rose, Lady-Luck, the twinz, etc.

I'm not always there
But you're always with me
I don't always miss you
Cause I see you all the time
You are in my sights
Each time I look in the mirror
I am what I am
Cause you are the ones that shaped me
I take you with me
Where ever I go
I've seen different things
      and met different people
That's why even though you all are a part of me
We are still very individual
With that said
Even though I am the only one
Who can be me . . .
U R Me, cause
Collectively
U All R a part of me

Nintendo (Tribute to Youth)

Double Dribble, Double Dragon, Dragon Warrior
Teenage Mutant Ninja Turtles, Wizards & Warriors
Street Fighter 2, Mortal Combat, NBA Jams
Duck Hunt, Paperboy, every single Mega Man
Tecmo World Wrestling, Abadox, Castlevania I & III
RBI Baseball, Metal Gear, Super Mario Trilogy
Mike Tyson's Punchout, Tetris, Dr. Mario
Bases Loaded, Tecmo Bowl, Contra, Battletoads,
Legend Of Zelda, Base Wars, Blades of Steel & Pong
Ducktales, 1942, Galaga, Donkey Kong
Blaster Master, Excitebike, Uncle Festers Quest
Royal Rumble, Shinobi, Pac Man were the best

This Life

This Life Is Inspired By People U Hate
This Life Is In Spite Of U
This Life Has No Timeline That Makes Sense
This Life Has Stolen From U
This Life Has Given 2 Him
This Life Could Care Less What U Think About It, Cause
This Life Knows It Did, What Was Best
This Life Heard Racist Comments Said @ Me
This Life Heard Racist Comments Said 2 Me
This Life Was Asked 2 Make Nuclear Weapons 2 Destroy The World
This Life Knows Way 2 Much Already
This Life Will B Gone Before Its Time
This Life Will Accomplish More Things Than U Can Imagine
This Life Can Get Deep Inside Your Mind
This Life Raised Kids Cause Their Parents Didn't
This Life Demands Attention
This Life Is 2 Late
This Life Is Right On Time
This Life Is Before Its Time
This Life Has An Unbelievable Story U Will Never Hear
This Life Disappointed U, Cause
This Life Wasn't Cooperating With Your Ambitions, Meaning
This Life Didn't Do What U Wanted It 2, Because Of That
This Life Will End Soon, But
This Life Will Never Die

I AM 2003

I am the spice that makes everything taste better
I am the elephant that keeps the lions in check
I am the stranger who hands you a rose when you need it most
I am the compliment that runs through your bones
I am the crash that leaves you confused & curious
I am the fire that warms you through
I am the venom that brings you back to reality
I am the antidote that gives you a fighting chance
I am the kiss that makes pain worthwhile
I am the whisper that makes you smile
I am the pack that hunts so smooth
I am the kid that speaks the truth
I am the plan that is thought to perfection
I am the plan that constantly needs to change
I am the future interesting but not strange

I'll Teach You The Most Important Thing You'll Ever Need To Know . . .

Thank You.
Why?
For Teaching Me What I Needed To Know . . .
As Important As That Was . . . It's Not What You Need To Know.
Then What Is . . .
Do You Trust Me?
Yes . . .
Discipline . . . I Want You To Challenge Yourself To Write These Two Words As Many Times As You Can . . .
Is A Hundred Enough?
Is That All You Can Write?
500? 1,000?
Can You Write More?
What Else Can You Teach Me? Algebra? Calculus?
Sure . . . But Write Those Words Some More . . .
Thanks For The Book You Recommended!
No Problem But Write Those Words Some More . . .
Thanks For Getting Me Out Of Writers Block.
Thanks For Helping Me With My Thesis.
Thanks For The Cooking Tips.
Thanks For Advice I Needed When I Was Really Down.
Your Welcome, Have You Been Writing Those Words?
I Finished An Entire Journal . . . Take It, I Don't Think I Can Write Anymore . . .
Not Bad . . .
I Need Your Help . . .
What's Wrong?
Times Are Tough . . . I'm Confused & I'm Feeling Down. I Don't Know If I Can Do This. I Feel Like I'm On My Own. I Don't Know If I Am Strong Enough? I Need Help . . .
You Can Help Yourself . . .
How? Can't You Give Me Some Advice?
You Already Know Everything You Need To Know About Your Self . . .
Please I'm Begging You . . . I Can't Stop Crying? I Losing Faith, In

Myself...
I Feel Like Nothing. When I Look In The In The Mirror, I See Nothing.
Someone Wrote An Autobiography, That I Think You Should Read ... It Will Tell You Everything You Need To Know, About Yourself. Here, Read It To Me ...
Who Wrote It?
Read It Aloud
Definitely Beautiful Definitely Beautiful Definitely Beautiful Definitely Beautiful
You Did ... Look In The Mirror Again ... Those Are Your Words ... Definitely Beautiful ... Never Forget It

YOU'VE BEEN SKETCHED BEFORE

I could, but I'm sure it's been done before?
Done well? I don't know . . .
But honestly done, for sure.
Cause there's been one written about you before . . .
A beautiful poem speaking you up, or
A beautiful poem tearing you down . . .
A beautiful poem talking you up, that makes you still sound bad, and
I'll have to walk away after reading it.
A beautiful poem tearing you down, yet
You still sound good, & I'll have to look closer.
Cause let's face it, when the last person wrote a poem about you . . .
It was either when they couldn't love you any more.
Or when they couldn't love you anymore?
When the poems about you were written,
It was either when they couldn't see any of your flaws.
Or when they had to point out every single one . . .
Either way I'll be able to read between the lines of that poem
I know you can never be as perfect, as your admirer makes you sound.
& you can't be as crazy and bad as your ex says in his 16 bars.
But I'll read between the lines of that poem. Whichever way it may go.
But where is your poem?
Someone out there wrote a poem about you before.
I know someone wrote a poem about you before.
Someone out there!!!—Wrote a poem about you before.
I wanna see it . . .
I wanna read it . . .
I want to read that poem.
I need that poem to read that poem.
Cause I want to read that poem.
I. Need. That. Poem.
I wanna read that poem.
So I can know, if I should leave you alone, or
If I should take the time to write my own.

My Favorite Poem

What is my favorite poem.?
What is my favorite poem.?
I could say it depends on the day.
I could say it depends on my mood.
A Favorite poem may stay the same
or change sporadically.
I could say it's the one I remember word for word.
I could say its poem A or poem B
Oh yeah poem 3 and . . . four too . . .
I could say it's this one or that one
It's a short one or a long one,
It's that one that describes red or blue.
That old one, or the one that's brand new.
Ones by Shakespeare, Frost or Langston Hughes
Hell that one by Dr. Suess.
But if you really want to know . . .
My favorite poem is the one written in my head.
The one I can't even put in words.
My favorite poem is the poem,
I think of over & over again . . . all day long . . .
My favorite poem is you.
Cause that poem makes me feel like, there ain't nothing wrong.

I Don't Wanna Write Today.

I don't wanna write today.
I don't wanna write right now.
I wanna read something today.
I wanna read something right now.
Speak to me. Read to me.
Tell me something.
Scratch that...
Tell me everything.
So I don't have to write it.
You write it this time...
Cause I don't wanna write today.

Someone asked me how to write. I wanted to laugh, because it is just something that's in you. It's in everyone. They said, "When I write it doesn't make sense." I replied "Then you must have just wrote something good." Sometimes it doesn't make sense to you, cause you don't think others will understand. But you'd be surprised. Sometimes you write something and it truly doesn't make sense. So what's wrong with that? The best way to write, is to write and not care. How do you write an Epic, Long Standing, Never Forget The Words Poem? Here's an idea. Read & then write whatever it means to you . . .

How To Write An Epic Poem

How do you write an epic poem?
You must start it with a thesis that has an original hypothetical dissertation
Then draw thoughts from your outline
Bring ideas to life to resurrect a dead metaphor
Where not even the subject can predict the predicate
Apply a wide vocabulary so you don't say things over and over again, or repeat yourself
    so you sound redundant
Use similes like, they were as important, as the concept
When you write an epic poem
Have a specific point to reaffirm
That's how you write an epic poem
You must antagonize with antagonyms
That makes the reader "mad"
So they don't know if the "goods" are "bad"
And after sifting . . . What's "apparent???" Is what's "left . . ."
& then "skim" the poem to "overlook" the point
To write an epic poem
Give the poem character by misspelling phonetically
Use another word for synonym
And define the word that rhymes with orange
That's how you write an epic poem
Remember in an epic poem
Antonyms are on the same side as Pro-Nouns
With mixed metaphors searching for their identity
Follow it up by a very condensed, shortened run-on sentence
So if you choose to write an epic poem
Use an irregular verb in a fragment so that it's more compact.
Talk about something horrible that had happened to make the past tense
Then use so much personal vernacular and "common" slang words you have to re-edit the
    mistakes by spell check
After that use an over-used cliché that makes the reader say . . . touché
Cause in an epic poem
The rough draft is better than the final copy, cause something epic is better "rough"
Finally when writing an epic poem, make the point to your argument,
That in an epic poem, you do not always need a definitive point, in your closing
statement.

                                            All poems written by,
                                            Doug Lemon